Queen

Women of the Miners' Strike

COAL

Queen
Women of the Miners' Strike
COAL

T R I O N A   H O L D E N

SUTTON PUBLISHING

First published in the United Kingdom in 2005 by
Sutton Publishing Limited · Phoenix Mill
Thrupp · Stroud · Gloucestershire · GL5 2BU

British Library Cataloguing in Publication Data
A catalogue record for this book is available from the British Library.

ISBN 0-7509-3971-0

Typeset in 12/15pt Sabon.
Typesetting and origination by
Sutton Publishing Limited.
Printed and bound in England by
J.H. Haynes & Co. Ltd, Sparkford.

DEDICATED TO THE COLONEL

With thanks to:
the women who volunteered to tell their highly
personal stories, WAPC, Sue Dempsey,
Mandy Little, Jim Frank, Joan Parker

Contents

List of Black and White Plates
between pages 112 and 113

Campaign Song

WAPC

We are women, we are strong,
We are fighting for our lives
Side by side with our men
Who work the nation's mines,
United by the struggle,
United by the past,
And it's – Here we go! Here we go!
For the women of the working class.

Introduction

Once upon a time, not such a long time ago, coal was the lifeblood of Britain. Dirty and smelly as it was, the veins and arteries of the nation ran black with it. Coal was the primary source of energy, it was the backbone of major industries such as steel, power stations depended on it, people curled up next to it in their homes, its existence meant work for large communities all over the country. It kept the nation alive from day to day, minute to minute. Coal was not an option, it was a necessity.

It wasn't by chance that it was known as King Coal, and those who carved the fuel from the ground were powerful, not only physically but politically. To carry on the corporeal metaphor, it had Britain by the 'short and curlies'. In the latter part of the last century there was no more feared union than the National Union of Mineworkers (NUM). Politicians dreaded the damage it could do and everyone, especially the miners, was aware of this.

Evidence of the miners' muscle came in the early 1970s. The strike in 1972 brought the country to a virtual standstill. The Conservative government was forced to declare a state of emergency as fuel supplies dwindled. A three-day working week was introduced. The miners were victorious; they won a deal that brought in fatter wage packets each week. The men walked out again in 1974 and created the same crisis, with power cuts and a nationwide paralysis.

Introduction

The strikes added to the headaches of a troubled Tory government. The Prime Minister, Sir Edward Heath, called a general election, hoping for a mandate from the nation, but the electorate wanted a change. Labour won and moved fast to do a deal that got the miners back to work.

It was against this backdrop that one of the most important chapters of contemporary social history in Britain was played out. In the 1980s, with the Tories in power once again, Margaret Thatcher's government was acutely aware of the threat from the coalfields. The feeling was that Arthur Scargill, the leader of the NUM, was spoiling for a fight. To weaken the miners' hold, fuel was stockpiled at power stations and the security services closely monitored political activists and union activities. Plans were put together to deploy police and the military in the mining areas during a strike. The battle lines were drawn.

The surprise announcement in March 1984 that Cortonwood Colliery, near Barnsley in South Yorkshire, was to close was seen by the NUM as a declaration of war. The pit had not been due for closure – in fact, millions had just been spent on the infrastructure at the colliery. Was it coincidence that Cortonwood was right in the heart of Scargill's home turf (he lived just up the road)?

For the miners this was an irresistible provocation. Arthur Scargill called for a walk-out – there was no national ballot. The men answered the call and downed tools. There are those who maintain to this day that, as there was no countrywide ballot, the strike was illegal and if there had been a vote, the majority would have wanted to give negotiation more of a chance. On the other hand, many involved in the dispute still believe support was almost universal, and they would have been victorious if it had not been for the 'scabs'. But all that is academic now. The strike happened, and lasted a year. It brought with it great hardship, violence and mutual hatred

2

between the powers that be and the mining communities. The scenes of civil unrest were among the worst seen in Britain in living memory. The miners and their families were branded as 'the enemy within'.

As the months passed with no sign of a resolution, frustrations grew. Families had their benefit payments cut on the basis that they were getting strike pay, which they were not. This meant people were struggling to put food on the table. It was a bitter winter and many could not afford fuel to heat their homes. Some eight months into the strike a few men started to return to work – this was in the run-up to Christmas 1984. By February 1985 more and more were breaking the strike and becoming 'scabs'. The men voted to return to work in March. Within months of the strike ending, collieries began to close. Cortonwood was among the first. With what appeared to be unwarranted haste, bulldozers were brought in to demolish the pithead buildings; in some areas it took under two years to erase the local pit from the landscape. No memorials were put up, no traces left of a way of life that had once seemed indestructible. It was a turbulent time which left deep scars. Communities were destroyed, families torn apart. As one former miner said to me, 'It wasn't what Thatcher did, it was how she did it. We were ethnically cleansed.'

The outcome of this watershed in British industrial history was to give the Thatcher government a powerful victory over a major union; it shattered the miners and changed industrial relations forever. In the ensuing twenty years most of Britain's pits disappeared, as predicted by Arthur Scargill. When the strike began there were 170 collieries with 180,000 miners. Today you can count the number of deep pits on two hands; they employ only a few thousand men.

I was one of the BBC's team of reporters working for radio news in the Yorkshire coalfield during the strike. At twenty-four I was their youngest national reporter. I had a different perspective from most, as I had experience on both sides of the front line. I would do my reports from the picket lines and be treated by the miners as the 'enemy without' – journalists were regarded as traitors, they were seen as part of the establishment.

With snarls and verbal abuse still ringing in my ears when I had finished my work, I would head for the other side of the fence. My younger sister lived near Barnsley and was married to a miner. They had a 3-year-old son and were struggling. I would stop off at a supermarket on the way to their house to buy them food. I witnessed the damage it did to real people, not politicians or union bosses who didn't know what it was like to go hungry. The victims were families like yours and mine, the silent majority who were generally law-abiding, authority-respecting souls. The strike changed that.

When you speak to people in the former coalfields you will encounter time and time again a deep-rooted anger towards the 'Establishment', especially the police. People complain that the tactics were heavy-handed and uncalled-for; the Metropolitan Police from Greater London invariably get the bulk of the blame. People say they will never forgive or forget how the men in riot gear treated them – not only the miners but also their wives and children. It is a distrust that persists to this day, and has been passed on to the next generation.

Having said that, not all the consequences of the strike were negative. Of particular interest to me was the impact on women in these communities. Women came out of the kitchen not with the idea of becoming political activists, but to support their communities. It was a spontaneous movement that occurred all over England, Wales and Scotland. Women saw it as a fight for jobs, and therefore a fight for survival. They were mobilised, transformed by a wartime spirit. They came from traditional backgrounds where women cared for the children and the home. They were groomed for marriage and motherhood; if they worked, it was in a mill or factory. They were not brought up to aspire to a career. They had strong opinions, but not for public consumption – they were expressed within their close circle of family and friends. So they were staggered when the strike came and they discovered they had a powerful voice. They would speak and people – their menfolk included – listened.

Their movement took shape early on in the strike when, angered by reports in the press that they weren't backing their men, the women decided to show they were behind them 100 per cent. They began to hold local meetings and organise food kitchens. As the momentum grew they formed into protest groups, coming together as Women Against Pit Closures (WAPC). The women orchestrated mass marches and rallies, they raised thousands of pounds to help mining families. They stood shoulder to shoulder with the miners on the often dangerous picket lines; they nurtured their communities with food and necessities such as clothing. Women who had once had difficulty writing were composing their own speeches and addressing huge gatherings. Their world had been turned on its head; the men viewed them with a new respect and gratitude. The Trade Union Congress formally thanked the women for their support, and acknowledged that without it the strike would not have lasted as long as it did. The women were contacted by protest groups from around the world, such as Chilean freedom fighters and peace campaigners. They were invited to speak in the Soviet Union and across Europe. Perhaps most importantly of all, in the chaos the women found qualities in themselves they didn't know existed. There is a neat symmetry in how they lost one community, but out of it created a new one, a sisterhood.

In this book I concentrate on the South Yorkshire coalfields because that was my home patch. I had lived there, knew the people and the terrain. I chose the women in Queen Coal from this area – some I knew at the time of the strike, others I knew of. I could equally have featured women from Wales, Scotland or other mining areas in England; the movement was widespread and action groups formed everywhere.

For some, the relationships that came out of these difficult times have outlived the coalfields. WAPC still exists. Its numbers have dwindled over the years, as have the number of pits, but it campaigns against closure of the few remaining collieries and for the return of King Coal. Far from letting go, these women have hung on to the spirit of 1984/5.

Each woman in this book was carefully chosen. I was looking for stories that represented the divergent outcomes for women. They all wanted history to record what could be achieved in times of great adversity. They all know of each other – a few of them are still in regular contact. They have told their stories with candour, honesty, sadness and humour. As my editor, Christopher Feeney, put it when he read the manuscript, 'It feels like a journey from darkness into light.'

CHAPTER ONE

End of an Era:
A Reporter's Tale

I am going to begin with an ending. It might sound odd, but bear with me and you will see why.

On Tuesday 26 October 2004 I sat in my car on the road leading to the last working pit in the Selby Coalfield in North Yorkshire. The site was signposted off the A19, the main road to York. It was an unseasonably sunny, dry morning, making the flat fields seem a little less boring; even the two power stations on the horizon had a Legoland feel to them. The plumes of smoke heavy with toxins were almost cheerful as they took on shapes of ships and animals against the deep blue sky.

It was what I call a Winnie the Pooh day – where the weather is so fine you believe nothing can be that bad or terminal. Only on this occasion the event I had come to witness was both those things, and its impact would be felt well beyond the uncluttered tracts of farmland that stretched as far as the eye could see.

I was waiting for the imminent arrival of a gang of 'angry' women. They were en route from South Yorkshire to protest against the closure of Riccall Colliery, the last of the five mines which had made up the UK's so-called superpit in Selby. It was only by chance that I happened upon this important slice of history. I was in Yorkshire interviewing women for this book, and my visit coincided with this true end of an era. Many of the women in the following chapters are or were members of

Women Against Pit Closures, a group made up of the mothers, wives, daughters and sisters of miners. It came into being shortly after the start of the strike in 1984/5. WAPC began in Barnsley, but other groups sprung up in parts of the country where there were coalfields.

It was while chatting to the remaining members of Royston WAPC that the call went out for them to rally round for a protest. After twenty years on the front line – their own kind of coalface – the members of WAPC were hardened to campaigns; it had become second nature for them to down tools – well, dishcloths and the like – and make their voices heard. I had been invited to come along and witness them in action again. The last time I saw them in full battle cry was two decades ago, so I was keen to see what had changed in that time.

Although I have reported on many demonstrations over the past twenty-five years, this event was different – I wasn't actually there as a reporter, I was recording events from a different perspective. Part of me felt like hopping on the bus with the ladies when it arrived; another part, though, fell back on the years of BBC training that had instilled in me the need to observe and not participate. I also had no idea how things would unfold. I was early – always am – and I watched as a police van drove by towards the main pit road. Shortly afterwards there was a Yorkshire TV outside-broadcast van in its wake. Then a number of boneshakers with tousled men inside – I deduced they were local reporters.

I was struck by the irony of the notice at the entrance to the site, which said 'Riccall Mine – caring for the future'.

I began to worry, as there was no sign of the women. They had been due forty-five minutes earlier. I called Kate on her mobile – they were lost somewhere west of the town of Selby. I gave them directions and, sure enough, fifteen minutes later they arrived in their rented mini van, all smiles and arms waving.

You would be forgiven for thinking that this coachload of respectable middle-aged ladies were really on their way to the bingo or a church bring-and-buy sale. They were all wrapped up against the cold in their smart sensible coats and woolly gloves. They had a stash of provisions – sweets and bottles of water – which they were happily sharing out while chattering away. They were a most unlikely band of insurgents – as it turned out, though, they were cats among clueless pigeons.

The small clutch of journalists hoping to squeeze a headline out of what most editors regarded as yesterday's news hung around the security gate. There were a few snappers from the local papers and a cameraman from *Sky News*. The word from inside the grounds was that the media were allowed in, but the women were most definitely not. Bridget Bell, who had organised the demo, was driving the van. She pulled over before the gate to have a quick word with me. I told her that it appeared they were not going to be allowed in – this prompted tutting from her and shouts from the back of the minibus. 'Who says we can't come in? We shall see about that. Do you want to come in the bus with us Triona?' But the bus wasn't going anywhere. A lone security man was making his way towards the women to try and talk them out of their mission. He never had a chance.

The barrier was one of those single white metal bars set across the entrance, with open grass verges on either side. It appeared to have been put in place more to give the guard in the plastic hut something to do by raising and lowering it, than actually to protect anyone from determined intruders. I felt a bit sorry for the guard, who was small, rotund and ruddy, like PC Plod in Noddy; he tried to use his short body to supplement the barrier, stretching out his stumpy arms in order to stop the women from breaching the perimeter. He was clearly unaccustomed to having to do anything more than wave familiar faces through his meagre barricade.

Bridget Bell – small with shortish blondey-grey hair and a keen intellect – was a pocket-sized Rottweiler. As the other women tumbled out of the bus, straightening their skirts and smoothing out creases on their coats, Bridget set to work on the guard. She was more than a match for him. He did his best trying to negotiate with her but, clearly, reasoning wasn't part of his job description. He became visibly agitated because the more he remonstrated with Bridget, the louder and firmer her voice became. She was like an angry schoolmistress telling off a naughty pupil who had let off a stink bomb. The group of journalists gathered round – ever hopeful of the confrontation coming to blows. Bridget pointed out to our roly-poly friend that he was 'one', whereas the women numbered 'twelve' and, in light of that, he couldn't physically stop them going onto the site. And anyway, they would be walking onto land that was part of the nation's heritage.

With that, Bridget dismissed him and waved to the women to carry on as planned. The guard stood back, open-mouthed and helpless.

The banners, which the women had first made for protest rallies in the 1984/5 dispute, were unfurled, and they walked around the barrier up a leafy drive, where a signpost said, 'Welcome to Riccall, UK Coal'. Chanting their fighting song, arm in arm, and doing interviews on the hoof, they headed towards the management HQ. It was quite a sight. The colliery was in the middle of nowhere – there were no houses nearby. The road leading up to it was landscaped, planted with pretty deciduous trees giving it the feel of a pleasant country park. Almost like actors, the women got into character. They stopped smiling and nattering, assumed angry faces, stiffened their backs and marched – banners in hand – towards the main colliery building. Their look of determination was impressive. Although I couldn't help but pick up a carnival feel to the occasion, the protest didn't have the desperate edge of many on which I have reported.

At the doors to the offices there were more local reporters and a few miners shuffling around in the background. UK Coal officials also made an appearance – although they didn't stray far from the doors. Perhaps they felt safer with an exit route behind them. Stabbing a threatening forefinger in the direction of the UK Coal spokesman, Bridget demanded to know why they would not be allowed into the building to attend a press conference. Why was the pit being closed down when there was so much coal beneath her feet – and at a time when there were warnings of power cuts in the coming winter months owing to fuel shortages?

She didn't get any coherent answers at this stage, but the photographers kept snapping and the cameras rolling. It seemed to me that having this moment recorded for posterity, even if it was only the local media, would be the most important achievement of the day. The women insisted that they would cheer the miners as they clocked off at 1300 hr, the last underground shift at Riccall. The NUM official at the pit, Maurice Kent, came out to mingle with the women and talk to the reporters. In a crisp, new, striped shirt and tie, he nervously put across the men's side of the matter. He disagreed with the company line that the pit was uneconomic and couldn't compete in the global market. He told everyone how there were more than 60 million tonnes of coal here, it would last for a hundred years, and yet the Labour government was turning a blind eye – it didn't want to know, despite the massive subsidies it had given the company over the years. It did strike me as the economy of the visually impaired.

But there was something more shocking to me. Here we were, witnessing the end of the coalfield that had been the hope for the future of the industry twenty years ago. Men were promised jobs for life; the coalfield covered 110 square miles – the size of the Isle of Wight. That coal was still tucked away underground, an untapped resource that would be sterilised –

Maurice's deputy told me that meant you couldn't get it out in future without massive cost and having to sink new shafts. Here we were, shutting the door while the horse was still inside. At a time when fuel was set to become a key issue again, I remembered the power cuts in the seventies – cutting off this domestic source of fuel seemed like mindless vandalism.

So where were the legions of protesters? Twenty years ago I had seen men in their thousands rampage like furious wild creatures around colliery gates, wrestling with the powers that be for the right to work down their pits – to provide the black fuel that fed the veins of our nation. Then they were ablaze with rage and indignation. Where had all the men gone? Where was the male passion? On this historic day, when 'King Coal' was about to be castrated, the menfolk were nowhere to be seen. Instead it was left to twelve women – the not-so-dirty dozen – to wave their neatly sewn banners and sing of standing by their working men, who were noticeable only by their absence. Who was standing by whom?

I asked Maurice where were all the union members? He had no answer. Then why weren't any politicians present? You could be certain that if you turned the clock back to life under Margaret Thatcher, you would have found the Labour Party here in force. He told me the local Labour MP had been at the pit early that morning and had told the men they should be grateful they had received 'generous' redundancy payments. And then he left. Maurice spat out the words in disgust. He said the payments were not generous and the men who lost their jobs would struggle. He said all this with much shaking of the head and looking at the ground. There was a hopelessness about him; the feeling was that the Labour government had abandoned the miners again, and there was nothing they could do about it.

Backed into a corner, UK Coal realised they would have to meet the protesters. So the women and two men from the

NUM were invited in to hear from the UK Coal public relations spokesman – but only after the majority of the press pack had been decoyed to another part of the pit under the pretext of seeing the last shift finish. The spokesman eyed me suspiciously and demanded to know if I was a journalist, but before I had to perjure myself the women piped up, 'she's wi'us love', and bundled me into the room with them. The subterfuge to keep the hacks and the ladies separate seemed pointless to me. There was nothing this man or his team could say that would change anything. There are organ-grinders and then there are monkeys; if you are confronted with the latter you might as well save your breath. I suppose they feared sparks would fly and reporters' notebooks would be scribbled on with good copy about UK Coal officials being harangued by the women.

He spoke of massive financial losses, geological faults that had only appeared after Riccall was opened and had led to the pit becoming uneconomic. There were maps and splodges of coloured areas with faultlines drawn on them. They might as well have been bingo sheets for all they meant. The women had their say, but it felt like they were pushing against a squidgy blancmange that would wobble here and there but had little real substance.

Matters were interrupted with the news that the men were coming out, and we had to hurry if we wanted to wave them on their way. We gathered outside the exit and waited. The rotund security guard was there, as were a few real policemen who stood to one side looking surplus to requirements. The women cheered, chanted and waved their banners when the men finally came through the double swing doors. But I counted only about thirteen men. I had expected dozens of angry, disillusioned, dirty faces. For their part, the handful of men seemed more embarrassed than buoyed up by the women protesters. They ducked past them and headed for the car park without a backward glance. I felt they were almost ashamed to be associated with a political protest even though it was, in part, for their benefit. My, how times had changed. The women were also disappointed – they had expected more men to come out, but the pit had been run down over the past two years until the only people working underground were part of a skeleton crew, simply biding their time until its closure.

At its peak, Selby, the most modern coalfield in Europe, consisted of five pits and employed 3,500 miners producing 12 million tonnes of coal a year. When Selby opened it was heralded by the government as a 'striking symbol of the rebirth of coal as a major energy source'. Now, with the last pit closed, the whole project seemed to me to be more like a stillbirth.

I have been down a pit – Thoresby Colliery in Nottinghamshire. It was well before the strike. I was part of a press trip, so everything was made to look shipshape and shiny, but even then I was staggered by the working conditions the men had to face. If you tried to start the coal industry today there would be a billion working directives that would prevent you sinking a shaft; families would protest about the appalling conditions men would encounter. The basic comforts taken for granted in most workplaces were absent. There were no toilets, just holes dug around a corner; food was brought down for the meal break in containers that clicked shut – it was called 'snap'. But as they ate, it would become laced with coal dust. The air was thick and cloying, filling the men's lungs. When I returned to the surface the exposed parts of my skin, like my face and hands, were black. For a day or so afterwards I could taste coal in my mouth. And I had only been down the pit for a few hours. What must the effect have been for the men who were down there day in, day out for years? At the coalface, conditions were cramped, with temperatures of 40°C or more. Danger was a constant companion, whether it was from the heavy cutting gear or from falls of rock. I wouldn't work down a pit if it was the last possible job I could do.

You could be forgiven, then, for asking why there was such a fight in the 1980s to retain the pits. Obviously the primary reason was economic – jobs were what put food on the table. And these were not the poor miners of D.H. Lawrence's books. Underground workers were earning good money – they could afford decent cars and one or two foreign holidays a year. But another important factor was the sense of belonging. Miners were in a club of their own. The danger they faced, the support they gave each other, translated into relationships that transcended the coalface. If you ask a former miner what he misses, he won't mourn the conditions, perhaps not even the money; but he will pine for the friends, the partnerships that grew from working together underground.

As we stood in a semicircle watching the men leave the pit for the last time, I shared the sense of sadness, but it was a sentimental emotion for me. I was moved at seeing a chapter of history close. My reverie was interrupted by some excitement as a few of the women demanded to be allowed to go to the ladies toilet. I wasn't clear what the fuss was about, but PC Plod insisted on escorting them into the premises. It was only when one of the women whispered to me that in the past they had locked themselves in the toilets to establish a sit-in that it dawned on me what they were up to.

In the end the women didn't bother – an indication of how lost a cause Riccall pit was. It was coming up for teatime and the ladies wanted to get home. As our Noddy PC shepherded us off the grounds – relieved that no one seemed to notice that the protesters had stormed the citadel – I thought here was a death that had almost gone unnoticed, like the funeral of someone old and forgotten where most of the benches in the chapel were empty, and not a wreath in sight. If it hadn't been for the women, I would have missed it too.

And that brings me to the miners' wives and mothers, and the reason for writing this book. WAPC was a group born out of conflict and fear twenty years ago, when Thatcher's army of police and soldiers came into their world. The battles ceased long ago, but the women didn't retreat. The pits went, as did many of the men, but the housewives never wholly returned to their kitchens. The death of their community led to the creation of a new one. It was of their own making, and remained as strong today as it was two decades ago. The events of 1984/5 changed the lives of millions of Britons – the ones who intrigued me were this group, who discovered a whole new world beyond the coalface. Women who were born into traditional roles were forced by circumstances beyond their control to break from those boundaries. There was no going back. For some it meant a painful ending, but for others there was a new beginning. I don't believe in 'happy ever after', but I do believe in embracing change. The key is to approach it with a positive attitude – after all, next to death it is the one certainty we have.

The ladies got back into their minibus, their enthusiasm for the cause undimmed by the lukewarm response from the men. They were unshakeable in the belief that it was important to make a stand. By now they had abandoned their grim faces and left the role-playing behind, reverting to warm smiles and teasing each other like the old friends that they were.

As they headed off back to Royston, waving to me and smiling, I had a 'pinch-me' moment. I was finding it hard to come to terms with how much had changed. Obviously, most of the pits had gone, but I had thought the spirit lived on. At that moment I began to doubt whether it did. It was as if the women were the last remnants of a bygone age. And that meant I was history as well. Were we the dinosaurs of our time? Where had the powerful testosterone-pumped men gone? I suppose by that time they would have got old; many would have retired or become ill, leaving the pits with or without the strike. But their sons would have taken their place, and yet on this day there were no sons of these men to be found. They were busy going to college or working in supermarkets, meat-packing plants or call centres. At the time of writing this, there were seven deep mines left in Yorkshire – the last remnants of a huge industry – and no one seemed to care, other than a handful of tenacious women. As I drove away from Riccall the thought occurred to me that, truly, the world of King Coal was dead.

I was staying with one of my closest friends, Sue Dempsey, who lives in the tiny village of Shelf, near Halifax. We'd been at school together in Bradford, at the grandly entitled St Joseph's Roman Catholic College for Young Ladies. In retrospect the name makes me laugh; if there was ever a misnomer, that was it. The convent school, headed by a mother superior who had a fondness for the bottle, was off Manningham Lane in what used to be the moneyed mill-owner end of town. But the rich folk had sold out long ago, leaving their big houses to be turned into bedsits and brothels. The area had become a red-light district. At the gates to our school we would face a barrage of abuse from the hookers plying their trade. Then again, the so-called young ladies had more to do with St Trinian's than the Blessed Virgin.

Sue's son, my godson Anthony, had kindly allowed me to camp in his room for a few nights, although he was a little annoyed that I left mascara marks on his pillows. I suppose that would have been hard to explain to the leggy girls he brought home from time to time. As I headed back to their house along what I am certain is Britain's worst motorway, the M62, I tried to pinpoint what it was about this particular story that had kept it in my mind for so many years. After all, I had spent my life travelling the world for the BBC, covering major news assignments. I had witnessed many powerful and disturbing events, such as bodies of children piled high in famines, burnt corpses of the victims of war in Africa, men flying off to their death in the Gulf, hijackings, riots, mass deaths from floods in Asia, a military coup, to name but a few. Yet none of these stories had nagged at me as much as the strike of 1984/5 and the women who were involved with it.

My husband, Professor Ian Palmer, is a renowned psychiatrist. When I asked him about it, his view was that I could relate to the women as I shared something with them. To figure out why this was so important I needed to consider what that common ground was; pursuing that route would give me the answers I needed. Of course he was right, as I am sure he would tell you, in spite of being such a modest man.

The answer lay in my teens. Up until then my life had been on quite a different track to the women in mining communities. I came from a middle-class, moneyed family. My father was also a professor of psychiatry, and my mother a psychologist. I am one of four children who were born into what should have been a privileged and stable home. When I was five we emigrated to the United States – my father was part of the brain-drain of British doctors in the late sixties. For a while we lived the dream. We had the big house, swimming pool, fast cars, and a lifestyle where poverty was a dimly understood concept read about in schoolbooks.

I'm not sure why we abandoned this life to return to Blighty, but family legend had it that Dad, who was number two at the Missouri State Hospital, had got too big for his boots. In whispers we were told that the mafia, who were heavily involved in the 'big bucks private healthcare system' in the States, had threatened him. He'd been told to do their bidding, but had said no. It sounds a bit far-fetched all these years down the line, and as my father is long dead I will never know the truth. As a journalist, though, I am fond of conspiracy theories, so the mafia tale gets my vote and will duly be passed on to my children.

I would say that our return to England was the single biggest disaster to hit our family unit. Somehow the whole tapestry of our lives unravelled. My father, whose work had been celebrated in the USA – he was even in *Who's Who* – came home to find doors shut. The close-knit medical profession closed ranks on him. I think if he'd had the chance to do it all again he would have preferred to deal with the mafia than the jealous, incestuous old-boy network of doctors in the UK. Rejected and disillusioned, he began to drink, and with that the poison of alcohol tainted all our lives.

His work as a consultant psychiatrist took him to Sheffield. and we had been living in the leafy hamlet of Nesfield, near Ilkley. We had come back from the States with enough money to cover the creature comforts. Our home was a huge stone-built villa known as The Hall. When the family upped sticks and followed Dad to Sheffield, I stayed behind to finish my schooling at Ilkley Grammar. I was just sixteen and found myself living during the week with our old gardener and his wife and going back to our new home at the weekends.

My parents bought a place in Denby Dale, near Barnsley. I loathed going back there, though, as their relationship had turned from bad to nasty. As my father drank, my mother withered. I would return to find myself walking into a domestic war zone. My mother was despairing and my father dangerous. I once found a stash of his whiskey bottles chucked over the dry-stone wall across the road from the house; there were so many they would have filled a recycling bin for glass. Alcohol brought out the devil in him; a paranoid demon. One Sunday he cut the phone lines to the house, picked up a carving knife and went after Mum, who was crying herself to sleep upstairs in their bedroom.

He repeated like a mantra how she had left the marital bed, and therefore was in breach of her wedding vows. I wasn't at home, but my little sister was and she tried to wrestle the knife

19

from him. She was only about twelve at the time. She did stop him in his tracks, but only after he had twisted her arm up her back and sprained it. From being the apple of his eye, she became little more than an obstacle in the way of some insane vendetta. Little wonder she looked for, and found, an escape route.

Of course my parents divorced. And of course it left both parties broke. My mother found herself living in a council semi not far from Denby Dale, in the heart of the coalfields. Fortunately she wasn't a snob and, despite the painful change in circumstance, she just got on with things – she must have slept more soundly knowing there was no longer a drunken sword of Damocles hanging over her head. The house had a large garden, but the property itself was tiny compared with what we were accustomed to. Inside, it was a squeeze, as the furniture, carpets and curtains we'd salvaged from The Hall were simply too big. It felt as though the doll's house had shrunk around the contents. The thick-pile Axminster wasn't fitted properly, and was climbing the walls; the huge dining table left no room to move the heavy, expensive chairs.

Who knows what the neighbours – mostly mining families – thought of these newcomers who drove flashy cars, ate off fine bone china using silver cutlery, and spoke with large plums in their mouths. But I seem to recall they were kind to my mother. She had a good pair of legs, and when she was bending over, working in the garden, the miners who were returning home from the pit would either lean over the fence and start a conversation or just wolf-whistle. That cheered her up a bit.

It was around this time that I got a job as an apprentice reporter on the *Sheffield Star*. When I look back I shudder at how pushy I was. If I met myself now as I was then, I think I would give myself a good slap. At seventeen I had decided that I would be a journalist, and that was that. The need to get a job and earn money put an end to any academic ambition I might have had – I turned down places at university and concentrated on making the team at the *Star* give me a job. In the end I think they gave me an apprenticeship out of exasperation. I was always popping into the newsroom to nag them about letting me work there. I was totally stupid, but driven by a hunger for the work. I am certain, in the 300 or so people applying for the two places, I must have been the most ignorant of current affairs, but I learned early that the saying 'bullshit baffles brains' was true.

It was on the *Star* that I got to know the coalfields. They were my bread and butter. I would visit the sites and interview families in the pit villages, or do features on the local schools. The only thing people loved more than having their picture in the local rag was seeing their child's face; it sold papers. And for me it broadened horizons and kicked off a relationship that lives with me to this day.

Meanwhile, my younger sister had found comfort with a local miner who was three years her senior. Getting pregnant at fifteen was her ticket out of a desperately unhappy family home. The words frying-pan and fire come to mind. My mother forbade her from marrying, but my sister took the matter to court and was granted a special licence; by then she was sixteen and their son was a few months old. They set up home in a council house in a tiny pit village. No one was shocked by such a young mother; teenage pregnancy was common. She did get a hard time though from her neighbours, not because of her age but because of her background. She had a posh accent and was seen as having airs and graces. From feeling cast out she became an outcast. I saw her as often as I could. I suppose I felt guilty that she had borne the brunt of our parents' messy demise. While I was gradually becoming less stupid at work and climbing the career ladder, she was stuck at home, a child looking after a baby.

When the strike came in 1984 she was caught up in the midst of it. At the age of nineteen my sister and her three-year-old son fell into the category of 'enemies within'. Her husband worked at Elmley Moor pit, near Barnsley. He came from a family of miners. By then I had secured a position with the BBC as their youngest national news reporter, and one of the few females to hold that job. I lived in a schizophrenic world where I would start the morning broadcasting on the main national BBC radio news from the violent picket lines, then move on to my sister's house nearby, via a supermarket, to bring food to keep her family from starvation.

This is a piece I wrote not long after the dispute ended. I've included it because it is like an entry in a diary written at the time.

On the 'Line'
by Triona Holden

I knew it was going to be bitterly cold on the picket line. What else could it be in the dead of a nasty January morning at Orgreave Colliery back in the strike of 1984/5. As I pulled on my stiletto leather boots my sensible inner voice warned that I would regret it, while the pushy, tarty, woman in me couldn't give a bugger. I was 24 and felt it was worth suffering a few chilblains for the sake of wearing heels and making my woefully short legs look a little longer. I knew it didn't make sense, the angry striking miners had more to think about at five in the morning, confronted by hundreds of riot police, than a young BBC radio reporter's pins. But then sense was never one of my qualities.

It was the same with the 'slap'. I got up half an hour earlier than I really had to just to get the eyeliner straight and allow time for the mascara to dry. For me my Lancôme Waterproof was as much part of my wardrobe as a pair of thong 'NVK's (No visible Knickerline). Once the make-up was on I checked that my Uher tape recorder and microphone were working. All in order I left the slumbering hotel to cover the arrival of coach-loads of 'scabs' at the pithead.

At the time I had just exchanged my bumbling old Beetle called Whizz for a racy MGB GT that was too grown-up for a name. The rubber bumpers killed it a bit but the engine roared loud enough to help me forget that failing. In retrospect it wasn't very clever driving up to the picket line in a sports car. The words 'red', 'rag' and 'bull' come to mind.

I drove as near as I could to the action. The pickets were corralled behind yards of metal barriers; in front of them were the police, arms linked and dressed for trouble. A coach was due any minute and I was in a hurry to ditch the car and record the uproar that would ensue. I was too busy struggling to get tapes and batteries from the passenger 'bucket' seat to notice that the barriers had been breached and the pickets had a new centre of attention – ME.

I tried to push the door open and met resistance; bodies were squashed up against it. When I did manage to get partly out of the car someone grabbed my arm and tugged me onto the muddy ground. In the ensuing scuffle clouds of hot tobacco-stained breath snorted into my face, words from many mouths told me I was in 'deep shit' and if I wanted to see this day dawn I'd better 'fuck off back to the gutter' I'd come from.

I wrestled to keep hold of my tape recorder, I'd somehow managed to press record and I was determined to have some 'actuality' of what was happening to me. I didn't have time to be scared, just angry and aware of a palpable hatred. The miners had been given an appalling press. I didn't blame them for regarding reporters as the enemy but I wanted to shout the fact that I knew where they were coming from as I came from there too. I had lived in mining communities since I was eighteen. It was unjust to attack me. I understood their fight; they'd got the wrong hackette.

But this wasn't the movies, and the action wasn't going to stop for me to make a moving speech about my sympathies for working men. Nothing could be heard over the sea of expletives.

In all the pushing and shoving I suddenly felt two steely arms grab me around my waist. My feet left the ground and I had lost control of my boot-clad legs. I was kicking and wriggling like a little girl as I was spirited away from the scrum. I was held so firmly that I couldn't turn my head to see who was manhandling me. I just hoped the BBC news cameraman was catching this fracas for evidence of assault. Once we were some distance from my personal angry mob I realised that I was shouting my head off like a lunatic. Somehow in the furore I had got the mistaken impression that I was bearing it in brave silence. Gob was not connected to brain at that point. I shut up and let myself be carried down a well-beaten track.

Some distance from the 'front line' I was dumped onto the ground in a field pockmarked with cowpats. Once freed I swung round to deliver some verbal abuse of my own. The 'rescue' meant I was missing the real action and thereby committing the biggest crime in the book: not doing my job. My unwelcome saviour was a sergeant from the Met, a particularly large sergeant from the Met. I tried to stomp my heeled feet on the ground in a rage, but failed to make much of an impact other than getting my foot stuck. I squared up to him as best I could but I was on shaky ground, as my nose was only level with his solar plexus.

'How dare you do that to me? I know my civil liberties and I have a right to be on the Queen's Highway unmolested. What's your badge number?' All textbook things journalists say to policemen who get in their way. I am not sure if any of it would wash in a court of law, but who cares; you have to have something to throw at them. The sergeant looked down at me in disbelief. 'You ungrateful cow, I've just saved your neck and you start spouting civil liberties.' He strode back towards the fray, only pausing for a Colombo-style parting shot 'And next time you might keep out of trouble if you try a bit harder to blend in; tarts aren't usually found standing on a picket line'.

His words stung all the more as my heels sank into quick-mud. I schlurped my way back to the road. By then my car tyres had been let down. Luckily I wasn't too late to witness squirming clutches of miners being bundled into police vans. They'd gone mad when the coaches carrying the scabs accelerated past them. The frosty dawn air was heated with fury; people were darting around in and out of the shadows. I recognised some of the other reporters who were being given a hard time – one had blood trickling from his nose. But they all kept close to the action, snapping at the heels of police and strikers, earning the sobriquet 'the pack'. I scurried around with them with my tape recorder, hoping to capture the war-like quality of the confrontation between authority and strikers.

When things began to calm down a bit and I felt I had enough material, I retreated to the safety of the other side of the road. I perched on an ancient dry-stone wall, scraped the muck from my heels, and with a shaking hand scribbled out my script for the seven o'clock news bulletin on Radio Four.

Once the *Today* programme heard about my narrow escape, they decided they wanted me to do a 'live' from the scene. This was to prove problematic. There were few women present at skirmishes like these, just a handful of miners' wives providing tea and moral support. On this occasion, as on the majority of previous clashes, I was one of the only female journalists on the other side of the fence, in the enemy camp. Inevitably I attracted more than my share of attention – again.

I decided to walk along on the safe side of the barrier, between the police and the miners, and wave my mike around to get what we called 'atmos'. The only trouble was that every time the miners caught sight of me they stopped shouting 'scabs' and serenaded me with a popular football chant especially adapted for the occasion. It went something like the song 'Leeds United, Leeds United, We'll support you 'til we die, we'll support you 'til we die', only the words had been changed to 'Get your tits out, get your tits out, get your tits out for the lads . . .'

I pretended to be one of the boys and laughed back at them to show it was water off this duck's back. But it meant that I couldn't do the classic live broadcast that started, 'I am standing here in front of . . .' To do so would risk ending up with a famous bosom and zero credibility.

With that in mind, I decided to do the broadcast from the radio car. I calculated that I would be unmolested locked inside the car. Headphones and lip-mike at the ready, *Today*'s studio producer told me I was next after the item on the heated row over whether or not 'groovy' should be in the *Concise Oxford Dictionary*.

Brian Redhead was just introducing me when I felt a lurch in my stomach. Odd for me, because I was generally too absorbed in what I was doing to be frightened of broadcasting live to 7 million people. But it was nothing to do with my nervous system. As Brian asked me to describe the scene around me, I looked up from the notes perched on my knee and the dawn had turned to dusk. I couldn't see out of the windows; the radio car was swaying side to side. There were so many men pressed against the car windows that they were blacked out.

BBC news saved money in those days by converting normal vehicles into outside broadcast units. On this occasion I was in an ancient Ford Escort estate that belonged to BBC Radio Leeds. I'd borrowed it for the national broadcast. The aerial sprouting from the roof of the car was at least 15ft high. It was a beacon calling all troublemakers to action.

They were rocking the radio car, attempting to turn it over. I tried to keep my voice steady during the broadcast as I explained to Brian how heated things were at Orgreave.

It wasn't easy to sound calm when any minute the car was going to do a somersault.

'So Triona, would you say the mood of the miners is hardening?'

'Well yes, Brian, I have seen dozens of men here bundled into police vans and of course that has enraged fellow strikers. They are also not keen on us journalists, in fact any minute now they are going to . . .' Click.

'Triona? . . . Triona? . . . It appears we've lost her. Let's hope she keeps her head well and truly down. Now, we have a special report on the growing number of pets whose owners take them to see a shrink, but is it really necessary . . .?'

Inevitably, the technology that could hardly cope with an ordinary broadcast had packed up under the strain. My line to London had gone dead; I couldn't even tell anyone that I was in a real fix. My heart was racing; the car was swinging from side to side like an unsafe fairground ride. I could hear feet on the roof. All I could do was try to retreat. I pressed a button to lower the aerial, there were shouts from above me as the spiky part at the top must have hit someone on the head. But it did the trick; with one last big shudder I felt them jump off the top of the car. The bodies started to move away from the windows. The men had found other quarry – a photographer who had been snapping away as they attacked my car, which made a particularly good shot as it had BBC written all over it in large letters. With the equipment stowed, I wanted to get out of the area fast. I put my foot down hard on the accelerator and drove out of trouble through the cordon of bodies. Did I hurt anyone? I don't know, and at that point couldn't care less.

A mile down the road I put the aerial back up and filed an updated report. I left out the bit about my car being attacked. I knew I would have to face this mob again in the coming weeks, and anyway who cares what happens to the reporter? I always felt I was there to observe, not to become part of the events.

Once the newsroom was satisfied that I had shared as much as I could with the nation, I headed off to my sister's house. She lived nearby and her home had become a regular tea stop after the many picket line clashes I had covered in the preceding weeks. Every time I drove to her house after a skirmish I was always knocked out by the irony that she was married to a Barnsley miner. One minute I was the enemy, the next I was the sister-in-law and auntie. Ben was only three. He had suffered dreadfully as a result of the poverty created by the strike. They had no money, little food, but worst of all no heat in the excruciating winter cold. The poor little lad had ended up in hospital with frostbite in his fingers and toes; the only good thing was that he was admitted and got a few days of proper food.

My sister was only a child herself; it was a harsh reality for a nineteen-year-old. She'd run away from her middle-class world and married a miner. Against the odds they had coped well, until the strike began and the wages stopped coming in. David worked at Elmley Moor Colliery: they had a two-bedroomed pebble-dash council semi. No one batted an eyelid at such young parents – it was common. Their home was in a godforsaken pit village called Clayton West. It was the kind of place where strangers were definitely not welcome. If you ventured out to the newspaper shop or local off-licence, the older women and men would stop you, fix you with an icy stare and pronounce, 'Tha's not from round here'. They were dangerous words, spat out as a warning.

My sister's posh accent and private school education meant she was regarded as a 'right stuck-up bitch'. Approaching her house you would run a curtain-twitching gauntlet. They all knew your business. Once again, the MG with its reinflated tyres would have certainly caused envy, and thereby trouble. My sister didn't mind; on the suffering front she'd reached saturation point, any more made no difference.

She had burned anything that was combustible in the house: her Scholl sandals, wooden salad spoons, books, old clothes, toys. She and Ben would go and scavenge for bits of coal in the slag-heaps around the pits. She'd taken a job looking after a local woman's children for £10 a week. It paid for some food, but she still had to steal potatoes from the woman's vegetable basket to make a meal for her own child.

Not surprisingly, after months of hardship the marriage was on the rocks. David was only twenty-one; he struggled under the strain of the strike. He had a family he couldn't support. They got a further £10 from the NUM's strike fund. Invariably it found its way into the till behind the bar at the local pub – David turned to alcohol for comfort. In the meantime my sister had run out of things to burn.

When I went to see her I would leave money, or arrive with bags of shopping. They were little contributions and in retrospect pathetic; I should have done more.

One day, towards the end of the strike, she had decided enough was enough. I helped her escape. I knew of a close friend's flat in north London that she could move into for a tiny rent. I helped with the deposit. It seemed a better option for her and Ben than the north of nowhere.

It was early evening when I arrived to spirit them away. By then the MG had been replaced with a hideous, sensible Austin Allegro, renamed 'all-agro'. David had gone to the pub as usual to spend what little he had on beer. We worked quickly as my nephew skipped excitedly along with us in and out of the house. The curtain-twitching was going strong, with him chattering loudly about what we were planning. We tried to shush him, but when you are three there is no such thing as secrecy.

Bundle after bundle of tatty clothes and sheets were crammed into the boot. The only precious thing my sister took that evening, other than her son, was her china. An assortment of old teacups and plates that she had inherited from our maternal grandmother. Of little real value, but for her they represented a rich past that she now hungered for.

We had to hurry just in case David returned home. He had already told her what he would do if she tried to leave him. It involved broken bones. After an hour or so of dashing about, we were ready to go. With the engine running, the little lad firmly strapped into the back seat, my sister pulled the door to her home closed, shutting off her recent miserable past. She got into the passenger seat, and with shaking hands lit up a fag.

The house was on a steep hill. There were two ways out of Clayton West. If we went down we could drive through the village and head for the M1. Going up meant a drive across the moors. As it so happened, my car was facing up the hill, and with so much stuff in the car I couldn't be bothered to do the three- or four-point turn needed to go the quicker route. It was a lucky decision. As I put my foot on the clutch and reached for the handbrake I glanced in my rear-view mirror and my heart leapt. Behind us, the bottom end of the road was impassable. David, his family and friends had formed a human blockade to stop our departure; they had expected us to drive towards them. There was a moment of suspense, when nothing seemed to move; the car and its contents froze to the spot; my sister let the cigarette burn between her red lips. All silence.

The pause was over in an instant. Twenty or more people were running up the hill towards us; I couldn't make out what they were shouting, but they weren't wishing us a pleasant trip. Their cries were an echo of the vehement chorus that greeted the scabs each morning, thick with coal-black hatred. I was more scared at that precise moment than of anything I had faced to date on the picket lines. It was a fear that was best left behind. My foot pressed down on the accelerator. With a surprised jerk, the car leapt up the hill; we headed up the road and away to London.

Covering the story was one thing, dealing with its impact on a personal level was another. It must have coloured what I had to say, but the passing of time makes it hard to be sure to what extent. There is one thing that still shines through the cloudiness of my memory: my family's involvement in the dispute broadened my perspective; it ensured an interest in the wider aspects of the strike and how it affected these people's lives. Unlike most of the reporters covering the strike who'd come up from the large news organisations in London, I didn't feel like an outsider. I wasn't from a mining family, but I had emotional connections.

As you can see from the piece above, I didn't have a dewy-eyed, romantic view of miners; I knew the reality. I wasn't with them come-what-may, but I did know them as people – not the men and women with savage faces of rage that were displayed on many of the news outlets each day and night. That was why I took time to get to know some of the women. I listened to what they had to say; I interviewed them about how they were coping, or not. I didn't demonise them or make them seem like total innocents. I knew they were a tough bunch who weren't scared of getting into a scrap. I had been on the receiving end of enough abuse from women as well as men on the picket lines to know how ferocious they could be. But that didn't apply to all of them; in fact that image represented the few. The many were just women who wanted to get on with being wives and mothers, and were terrified that their husbands would lose their jobs, leaving the family with no money. As often happens, the media was brilliant at thumbnail sketches showing extremes, but often rubbish at giving an accurate representation of the less dramatic, broader picture.

As the years passed I kept in touch with the women, and likewise some of them followed my career as I moved on to BBC TV as a correspondent and newsreader. I tracked the changes in their lives. We developed a 'history' that could only come with time. Not only could I identify with them through having lived among them but, like me, they had found their lives torn apart by events beyond their control. In my case it was the decline of our family that pushed me out into the world alone at a tender age; their security was taken from them with the end of the coalfields.

One of the few benefits I have found about getting older is that you realise clichés are not simply annoying sayings, but have their foundations in truth. My favourite is 'what goes around comes around'. Isn't it wonderful when you actually hang about long enough to see this in motion? The Buddhists know how to put us all on a level; it is an elegant philosophy . . . *how you live or have lived your life has a direct bearing on the quality of your future life or lives.*

Forgetting the reincarnation aspect of Buddhism for a moment and concentrating on the dishing out of justice, you can see this philosophy in action in the former mining communities. The women say their 'public enemy number one', Margaret Thatcher, is a case in point. As she wiped away tears when she got the sack as Prime Minister, the mining folk felt they had the last laugh. They delight in the thought that the property boom, nascent in the Thatcher years, has benefited their communities. It has meant that the more historic and traditional pit villages have become gentrified. The humble homes that miners struggled to hang onto through the strike are now worth many times what they were in 1984/5. They had no idea that they were sitting not just on coalmines but goldmines, as well. And what a twist of fate that this good fortune is down to policies championed by the woman who, they feel, tried to destroy them.

There is one village, Elsecar, where it is now virtually impossible to buy a house – estate agents have waiting lists of people wanting to live there. It is also the time when many people have come to the end of their mortgages; the bricks and mortar belong to them and their families. Some miners used their redundancy to pay off the mortgage years ago. It just goes to show that, no matter how bad things seem, the one certainty is that they will at some point improve. They might get worse before they take an upturn, but if you hang on long enough better times will come.

The women in this book are living proof of this. As one of them said to me with a wry smile, 'My life's been up and down more often than a whore's drawers; I'm not complaining like, only I never got paid.'

CHAPTER TWO

Going Back:
Denise Fitzpatrick

They say you should never go back, but a part of me had never left Yorkshire. Echoes of the place were always there in the back of my mind, persistent and audible. Although in the years since the strike I had returned to the area to visit friends, I had not been to the coalfield sites where I had worked as a reporter. As I drove up from north London I had a fixed idea in my mind what the place would look like. It resembled those shaky black and white images you see of early film footage. Over the years my mind had warped the reality and given me a romantic cliché to hang onto. I envisaged a landscape with idle collieries dotting the horizon, placards erected to commemorate the 'great struggle' of 1984/5. I had no doubt that rediscovering the scenes of so much drama would be easy, as if the cries of the pickets and police still reverberated across the Dearne Valley and would point me in the right direction. I was wrong of course, but I wasn't prepared for how wide of the mark my imaginings were.

Leaving the M1 at junction 36, heading for Rotherham, took me onto a pristine dual carriageway. It was so new, the tarmac shone black. It was like a huge child's racetrack that had been taken out of the box and assembled in a hurry. This mini-motorway had the grand title, The Dearne Valley Parkway, a name that meant business. It conjured up the image of juggernauts thundering along the road, heading for pulsing industrial sites, and fast-moving cars ferrying folk to their important jobs.

But this pretentious road was not troubled by heavy traffic. Few vehicles competed with me for a place in the slow lane. Opened in 1998, the 8-mile tongue of black was part of a regeneration scheme. The plan was to attract business to this economic desert. You could tell there were great expectations by the number of roundabouts they had built. There were plenty of signs announcing industrial parks this way and that, but there were, as yet, no roads to take you to anywhere, just tracts of scrubland with sleeping bulldozers waiting for the call to dig. Looking across the valley, I could see no sign of the retail promise being realised; sheep grazed on what should have been a new land of plenty. The road cut through stretches of barren land that appeared to be good for nothing. It was like a building site where the cash had dried up, the developer had gone bust, and the whole thing was left with rubble and broken breezeblocks.

The little roundabouts became annoying after a while; they seemed pointless, and meant the road had erratic turns for no reason, like a deranged snake. I wondered if the builders were showing off their roundabout-making skills, as if anyone was going to be that impressed with driving around in circles. After a few miles I began to wonder if I was in the wrong place. There were no landmarks – not a hint of a colliery anywhere. I recognised a few of the sheep, but nothing else. Perhaps I should have come off the M1 at the next junction. I was peering at the signposts looking for anything that might give me a clue as to where Cortonwood Colliery might have been. At last I came to it: a sign that proclaimed 'Cortonwood Retail Park'.

Following the roundabout with renewed purpose I found myself heading towards a huge Morrison's supermarket. There was an equally vast B&Q DIY outlet next door. As I drove into the carpark with its carefully manicured flower-beds full of delicate trees, I tried to get my bearings. There was nothing to say that a colliery had stood there; I was genuinely surprised. As I wandered around the site in disbelief, I couldn't detect the slightest trace of the pit – not a lump of coal to be seen. If I had not known for a fact that this was the exact location where I witnessed fierce fighting between police and pickets, I would have been lost. You would never guess what lay beneath.

I cast my eyes across the landscape, looking for the telltale winding gear of the other collieries that used to stand out like beacons. The metal towers were the hallmark of the industry. I had expected many of them to be gone, but I wasn't prepared for their total absence. Even the most powerful binoculars wouldn't have given me any clues as to where King Coal used to hang out in this valley that was once a stronghold. How could sites that were so huge be wiped from the memory of the terrain? Not even the pockmarks to hint at the digging and scarring of the land. I know twenty years is a long time, change is inevitable; but nothing remained, not a pithead office block, no baths, no roadways, not even a signpost to give you a clue as to where the pits used to be. I couldn't help but feel that Thatcher had done a pretty impressive job of wiping the collieries off the face of the earth. My eyes still searched for something that would tell the tale of such a recent history, but I couldn't even make out the slag-heaps that once stood like hunched sentries around the collieries.

I wandered into the cheap clothing/home store, Matalan, which was based in a warehouse big enough to accommodate a few jumbo jets, clean and climate controlled; I could have been anywhere in our Western world of retail, even a shopping mall in Florida. Nothing spoke of heritage. Most of the shop was deserted; the only hive of activity was at the checkouts where queues of people had fistfuls of £1 T-shirts and £5 jeans.

How the miners of the eighties would have delighted at being able to buy clothes so cheaply in their times of hardship, although they would have recognised the real cost of having such places on their doorstep.

It is probably just me being a romantic, but I came away from the site feeling a bit numb. This bland world of piped music and mass-produced goods being purchased by blank-faced zombies was not what I had expected. The characters couldn't be all gone. Where were those people who embodied the singular nature of the mining communities, good and bad? I realise there was nothing cuddly about them – they weren't pretty faces burnt on my memory; but I missed the strength and vitality that set them apart from the mundane: hard men and women who lived by their own rules. There would be those who had died in the last few decades, and those who had moved away, but there must also have been the survivors.

Half a mile up the road, on a hill overlooking the retail park in the village of Brampton, where the majority of the Cortonwood mining families used to live, I found what I was looking for: the remnants of a way of life that was passing into the history books; the last vestiges of a world that was being forgotten.

Denise Fitzpatrick, a woman of irrepressible energy, is every inch a part of that history. Two decades down the line, she is still up for the fray, fighting for those around her. Sadly, she is on borrowed time. The doctors have given her five years to live – she has a congenital heart disorder that has already claimed many of her siblings; although I don't think she would have any patience with pity or sympathy. She is a woman who has lived each day, and has no regrets and no great longings or desires, other than to see her grandchildren grow up. As with so many of those left in these shrinking communities, she often spoke of wanting to put down her tales in a book. Here are a few to be going on with.

The 'Cortonwood Comeback' is probably the last 'soup kitchen' still open after the strike. When the dispute ended many of the kitchens closed within hours, the women and the men fed up to the back teeth with the meat and two veg that had sustained them through the toughest year of their lives. If you eat the same food day in, day out, you can develop a lifetime's aversion to it, no matter how good it is, especially when it is served up with lashings of hardship. The 'Comeback' has had many roles to play over the years. Its primary aim has been to provide food, warmth and a place to have a good chinwag for villagers of all ages. It's just off the main road through Brampton and inhabits the tail end of what looks like a derelict Methodist church.

When I first drove to the community centre to meet Denise, whose determination helped set up The Comeback in the first place, I was surprised at the condition I found it in. The site was run down, with rubbish strewn about. Windows were barred or broken and part of the dwarf wall around the building had been knocked down. It wasn't the welcoming façade of a thriving community centre that I had expected, but then in this part of the world things often weren't what they seemed. If you wanted to get a clear picture of what was going on you had to take the time to get a closer look.

Knowing this, I persevered as I picked my way around the old chapel building, trying to find confirmation that I was in the right place. Eventually I spotted the Cortonwood Comeback sign over a back entrance that looked as if no one had stepped through it since Arthur Scargill was a local schoolboy living a few streets away. But through the thick, grubby glass I could make out some lights on inside. Sure enough, with a great push and shove I managed to get the door open. I followed the sound of voices. The place had the smell of disinfectant and school, but there was also a feeling of cosiness. The dark brick walls and tiled floor rang with the clatter of my stilettos.

Through a large inner door I found Denise Fitzpatrick and
her team of congenial ladies, aprons on, busily giving local
pensioners a hot meal. Immediately the impression of neglect
vanished, to be replaced by an atmosphere of care and
capability. The air was full of jokes and teasing. That was how
Denise liked it to be; her tonic for life's woes was laughter. She
was without doubt the one in charge, the mistress of this
domain, equally as popular with the pensioners as she was
with her gang of volunteers.

Denise was a woman who carried her big personality well.
She was only little, in height at least – less than 5ft at a guess.
But she had a full figure crowned by a generous, motherly
bosom. Her hair was as white as Andy Warhol's – your eyes
were drawn to the spiky halo. Denise would certainly have
stood out in a crowd, despite being vertically challenged. She
might kill me for saying this, but she put me in mind of the
group of lady dancers called the Roly Polys, who used to
appear on television alongside the comedian Les Dawson. She
had that feel of being a ball of energy.

Denise liked to keep those around her happy. She was a
natural entertainer, but she also had a quick wit that was to
come in handy when she took on figures of authority, which
she did often. Like so many women, she was changed by the
strike, but her metamorphosis was different to most. When the
NUM called out its men she was already au fait with how
unions functioned. She had worked in a car battery factory in
the late seventies, then in 1980 found herself pushed forward
by the other workers to be their representative when they
decided to join the Transport and General Workers Union. It
was a poisoned chalice, as the firm was against allowing a
union to be set up. I imagined it was like a scene from a
comedy film where a line of soldiers are asked to take a step
forward to volunteer for an unpleasant mission, and the whole
line bar one takes a step back. That one left to do the nasty job

would be Denise. Not that she would shrink from the challenge; she loved nothing better than a good cause.

As the daughter, wife and mother of miners, Denise was caught up in the thick of things during the dispute. That year she found herself stretched to the limit. She had a job as a cleaner at the NCB laboratories, where they continued testing to ensure the pits remained safe during the strike. The local NUM officials decided that as she was a member of the T&G she could go in to the site so long as she didn't cross any picket lines. At home she carried on doing all the chores, and with what time she had left she threw herself into the business of supporting the strike by helping with the soup kitchen, going on rallies and raising money.

It sounded like an exhausting and stressful time. Some of the stories Denise told revealed that there were moments when she reached the end of her tether. Then again, listening to her speak about that twelve-month period it was clear that, hard as it might have been, it was still the best time of her life; so much so that when it was all over and most people tried to settle back to what was left of their lives, Denise couldn't bear to let go. There was no way she was going to return to being simply a wife, mother and cleaner. She'd had a taste of a different world where she was needed by the many and not just the few, and she thrived on it. Denise performed best to a crowd, she had found her audience and, like many entertainers, she loved the sound of applause too much to walk away from it.

That is how Denise became instrumental in establishing Cortonwood Comeback. It was a centre aimed at the whole community, particularly those most in need, such as single parents, the disabled and the elderly. It was a continuation of the work started during the strike, in that it provided food and a place for people to meet and talk. It was a home away from home, a sanctuary from hardship, even if only for a few hours.

41

It struck me that in this feisty little lady you had a woman who wanted to be everyone's mother. Her passion was to nurture those around her. The end of the collieries and the need that it created were the perfect environment in which Denise's abilities could be put to good use.

When strike started, to be honest with you, I never thought we would have lost, truly I didn't, I know people thinks it's stupid but up to week before we stopped I never thought we would not win.

At end of strike I thought bollocks there's no way am I going to let everything go. Most of women I will admit they went back to what they were, not 'cos husband says 'No you're not going out', but because that were what they wanted. I've always gone out on day trips with me mother, it were a way of life. You only got a day out occasionally you used to save up and go to races for a day, simple things a lot of people took for granted we saved all year for.

I don't like to say it because it sounds like I'm cleverer than everybody else, and I'm not, but I knew, I knew as sure as I were breathing, as soon as it were done that life as we'd known it had finished, that's the only way I can put it to you, I knew that day that it were end of everything I had lived for all my life. I'm sorry, it still upsets me.

There was a moment of silence as Denise struggled with her emotions. Recalling that time was painful. The pits were not just a workplace, they represented a way of life, so when they went it was like a bereavement, and the grieving continues to this day.

There's only a few times in me life I ever had that really, really bad feeling. Once were when we buried me nephew David, he were just nine, we were very close, and then there were this. The next time I ever felt like that were when me mam died.

Big picture were my life as I'd always known it were finished and I thought, Oh no they're not gonna do this to me. Nobody's gonna take everything away not just for this twelve months. It were all I'd ever known all me life. So I got a few women and I says 'We're gonna have to do something.'

'What do you mean?' [they said]. I says, 'We're gonna have to do something 'cos you know there's going to be nothing,' I says, 'honestly there ain't.'

They says, 'Well what can we do?' I says, 'We'll do what we always do, we'll find somewhere for us all to go.' 'Cos it were all a strike centre you see, up parish hall they were doing parcels, wherever there were a gang of women you were there; somebody's house, you were there.

I says, 'We're going to do what we've done'. I says, 'We're going to be there and when nobody's got anywhere else to go they're going to come to where we are.' And I says, 'We're going to do it, we're going to do a community centre.' They says, 'Well how can we do that?' I says, 'We're going to,' I says, 'we are'. And we did.

Denise's husband Barry, a former miner, says life changed for the whole family as his wife became actively involved in charitable work and politics.

When police started pulling walls down and there were police throwing great big walling stones under cars, and ruddy soldiers there in uniform, soldier's uniform not police's, and they raced us all over bloody village as we were trying to get out of way. Well they got away with that without a thing being said, and I says to Denise, 'We've lost this strike, love.'

I lost strike and I lost me wife as well, 'cos she just started campaigning for this that and other, when Wapping came up she were there organising T&G to go down. She knew we were going to lose this community, not just pits and jobs.

43

There had been some talk before the strike of setting up a facility in the village for the community. With the help of the local vicar at the time, Nick Jowett (known as Nick the Vic), and the diocesan unemployment minister, the plans were put in motion. The local Methodist church offered to give the group access to a disused schoolroom. They even loaned the money to have the place renovated.

> I'm the same as everybody else, I really am a big believer in God. I don't like to say this but I'm as big a Christian as anybody that goes into a church, and I'm not saying that to brag, but you don't have to go to church to want to look after people.

It was a testament to the determination of Denise and the other volunteers that the centre still functioned after all these years. It had the feel of a venture flirting with bankruptcy, only kept going by the sheer doggedness of a handful of women. It had offered many services over the years, from dishing up hot food to unemployed men and women to hosting a fitness club. These days the centre was mostly catering for pensioners, providing a cheap hot lunch and somewhere warm to socialise. The place was run on a shoestring, money coming from donations and fund-raising. Actually, it was remarkable that it existed at all.

Denise was not one of those people from whom you had to tease information. She could speak ten-to-the-dozen, and I silently thanked God I had a tape recorder with me, as my shorthand could not have kept up. The only time the animated narrative stopped was when she threw back her head and laughed at her tales. On the occasions I met her it was always the same, although when her husband Barry was on hand he would try to cut in whenever she took a breath.

The stories came thick and fast. A favourite was about a rally in London during the strike when Denise was made a steward. It was one of the marches where people from all walks of life turned up to support the miners. It was a hot summer day, and one of Denise's group fainted in the heat.

> One of our team passed out so I had to wait with her to get transport to where the speeches were to be. When I had sorted this out I dropped back into the march behind the first banner passing by. It were a common cause so it didn't matter who you were with, we were all in it together. My experience was that people at these events were always friendly so I didn't think anything of it when a few of the ladies in the group started giving me friendly kisses. We were all laughing and joking. I did notice that there were people in pairs and they were of the same gender, and that made me wonder, but it was only when I walked in front and looked back at their banner that I realised what was going on. It said 'Gays and lesbians support the miners'.

Being kissed and cuddled by a group of lesbians was something of an education for Denise. In the mid-eighties homosexuality was still very much in the closet, especially in macho Yorkshire. Denise was aware of gays, but had never knowingly spent any time with them, especially lesbians. She had no problem with the group, and saw the funny side. But as she walked ahead to catch up with her own ladies she decided not to say anything to them, as they might not understand.

She got on with the business of demonstrating. Her group was hungry, so they left the demo to occupy a bench and have some lunch. As they ate their sandwiches they watched the parade go by. Denise's heart sank when she saw the Gay and Lesbians banner. She hoped they wouldn't spot her – but Denise was unmistakeable, with her short white hair. Her new-found friends whistled, waved and blew her kisses. For a moment the other women in Denise's party were puzzled, until it dawned on them that this was where she had got to when she went missing. Far from being shocked, they fell about laughing and spent the rest of the day teasing Denise about her 'letz-be friends'.

There was cackling from the volunteers at the Comeback centre, who had been listening to Denise recount this tale. They must have heard the story a hundred times, but it didn't wear out with the telling.

I have never lived it down, but it is only a laugh. The important thing was it showed me that they were just people like the rest of us and they were giving us their support. That were one of the great things about going on these rallies and demos, you went to places you would never have gone to and got to know lots of people and understand their point of view. The gays were some of the nicest and most sincere supporters we met.

Events like that march were an eye-opener for Denise. She realised there was a whole world beyond the tiny villages that were her home turf. She was brought up in poverty, one of thirteen children, although only ten survived past infancy. Their father was a miner, her brothers were down the pit. Mining was an integral part of her life. She had never known anything different. She lived out the preordained path followed by the majority of women from similar backgrounds.

This was her inheritance. Although her family were desperately poor, she says she had a happy childhood under the powerful and loving influence of her mother, a woman who would share what little she had with those in greater need. Denise's father was at Manvers colliery; working down the pit destroyed his lungs. She says one of her earliest memories was of her father sitting on the bottom step outside their house struggling to catch his breath. Denise says he had emphysema and today might have lived much longer as he would have been treated for it, but fifty years ago there was no effective treatment for him, no oxygen mask to help his breathing. He died at the age of 51. Denise was just eleven years old. Five of the children in the family were still at school, although the older boys were working down the pit by this time, so money was coming into the house.

We were poor but we weren't rough. We lived in village near here called West Melton. You know these days you read about toilets up yard – well we had it, we lived it. We had only the one outside toilet, no running water, nothing, no bath, no nothing. We did have electric but I were 14-year-old before we had a television.

We were really, really poor, but it were lovely – I wouldn't change my childhood for anybody's. I had a lovely family, brothers and sisters and aunties – well, I had two or three nice aunties. Me mother were one of 17 and every one of them lived.

Denise was the second-youngest and had an aptitude for schoolwork. She passed her eleven-plus and was offered a place at grammar school. But she refused to go, because none of her friends were going. Instead she went to technical college to learn shorthand and typing, hated it and soon used her intelligence to concoct ways of playing truant.

When I were thirteen I either had to go to grammar school or to technical college, so that were lesser of two evils, 'cos this other girl Pat were going as well. I hadn't been brought up with her, but we were pals. She weren't poor like us, but she had a bastard of a dad. I learnt shorthand not very good but I can type – not fast, but I can type. I never wanted to do owt, and when I left school you had to have a job before you left if you were at a technical college, you couldn't just leave. I went and got a job at Bolton sewing factory. Pat and me left school, we hated it. We used to play wag [truant]. We were always wagging it. Me mam hit the roof when she found out I'd left tech.

At sewing factory I didn't even learn to sew, I can't bloody sew now. I never learnt to sew, I just went, all me mates worked in mills. We used to have to get up 5 o'clock in morning, get on bus at quarter to six and come home 6 o'clock at night, and I were as happy as pig in muck, everybody were. I were earning £3 17 [shillings] a week. I used to give it all to me mam.

Then I met Barry. I were only seventeen when we got married. That were forty years ago. What did me mother-in-law say? 'Six bloody weeks, six month.' Well, she didn't talk like us, she were posh his mum. She said it'd never last, he didn't know what he were letting himself in for. And that he would be back, 'cos they were posh and I weren't.

Barry and Denise worked as a team through the bad and good times. Between them they have not only brought up their own five children but managed to give time and energy to other people. It is something they continue to do today, despite having to deal with their own serious health problems.

Looking at them together now it is impossible to imagine them any other way, but forty years ago things were different. Barry had trouble persuading his parents to let them marry in the first place. At the time they were both very young, and Barry's mother was fiercely against the union. Denise came from a very poor family, whereas Barry's parents were more well-to-do – still working class, but saw themselves as better than Denise, who was brought up in a hand-to-mouth world.

[Barry] My mum were a Londoner, cockney bleeder. Me and Denise decided to get married after we'd known one another six month and I'd come to live over here 'cos I got a job. I went over with a consent form 'cos you had to be twenty-one then to get married, you know, without consent.

I were 19. And they wouldn't sign it. Then just after Christmas we went over and asked them again and me mother says 'No, I told you I'm not signing no form until you're 21'. I said 'You don't need to sign it when I'm 21'. I said 'Well I'm asking you sign, I'm in a good job and I'm earning good money', which I were. I were earning a lot more than some other people. I were plate-laying, laying rail tracks and that, and I says, 'I don't want bairn born bastard so if you don't give me permission I'm going to court and asking court's permission to get married.'

Dad looked at me and he said, 'And would you do that Barry?' I said, 'Yeah I will Dad', I says, 'She's pregnant, I want to marry her, not 'cos she's pregnant, you know that 'cos I asked you before,' I says, 'but if you ain't giving permission I'm going to courts.'

So he says, 'Pass consent form', and he signed it, passed it to me mother, and she said, 'I'm not bloody signing it.' My father never lost his temper a great deal, and he never swore, but when he spoke his word were law. He picked form back up, gave it to her, looked at her, 'Joan I have told you to sign that form.' That were end of world, when me father said things like that – that were it.

Barry's mother did as she was told, and the pair were married. Barry switched from plate-laying to working down a pit. Like her mother, Denise got pregnant easily – they had five children in seven years.

Them that weren't pregnant when they married in years gone by didn't go to altar in white 'cos they'd never had sex, it were 'cos they were bloody lucky. He used to take his trousers off, throw 'em on bed, and I were pregnant before he got into bed.

Its true, some people are, I always remember me mother telling story when I were older about a new nightie. Me dad must have been still alive at that time. She went down to get it from Fords. It were Mr Ford says to her, 'Have you seen these, Mrs Holton?' He says it's brand new out, they've just started making it for nightwear. And it were this posh bri-nylon, brush nylon, whatever it was, and me mother says she looked at it and said "Bloody hell, I've had 13 kids in flannelette. What do you think I shall have if I start wearing that?'

The contraceptive pill had not been developed at that stage, so couples had to take their chances or use condoms, which were expensive. Barry said:

At that time to buy a packet of Durex they were 3s 9d and there were three in a packet. I went to barbers and it were one of lads that were new had just opened a shop up, Clive. So I goes in, has me hair cut, it were about four month after we'd had our Paul. He says, 'I've got to get some new Durex in, Barry'. [I says] 'How much are they', he says, 'I'll say £2 a box', so I bought a box. Telling her about it, I says he had this box of Durex, they're cheap, I bought whole box, save us running up and down, but she says, 'Well it's too late for that.'

When Denise speaks of her own mother, you can see what a powerful positive influence she was. Over the years she has emulated her mum. She didn't have as many children, but she was just as happy to open up her home to anyone in need.

My mam's name originally were Mary Levitt and she told me her mother were a gypsy. She says, 'Do you know, Denise, when we were kids we never knew where we were going to be living'. I mean, they lived in Brampton at one period, but not in one house, in about six houses at different times. They were building houses and every time they built a street me mother's mother moved into it.

Me mother said that when she got married and had kids – she used to say, 'But I didn't know I were having that bloody many . . . once I got a home for my kids I would never, ever move again', she says, 'cos we were just like gypsies – we've lived all over. And she were as good as her word, she didn't move.

They got married and went into lodgings, 'cos in them days even when we were young if you got married and you didn't have nowhere to live, well you had lodgings. You moved into a room in one of your family's houses – you know, shared kitchen – and had your own room and it were always done. They moved in with me Uncle Harry, my dad's brother. Then they went back up to Staffordshire where me dad had come from and they couldn't get no work up there so they came back and they lived with me Uncle Harry again, and then this house come empty on York Street and me mam went round and got it and she never moved no more and she could have moved loads of times.

There were three bedrooms. We were lucky 'cos we lived next door to entry [an alleyway where the first floor is built over it], they were all two-up and two-down unless you lived over big entry you see, and then that house had three bedrooms upstairs. So we were well off in that respect.

It were owned by a private landlord, Pat Choirbull. She was Irish and never did no repairs or anything, you know, it were falling down. One time family were sitting playing cards and the door between kitchen and front room come off hinges and flattened me mother onto table. There were a deathly quiet and then me mum says – and when she were mad she used to call you a bleeder – 'Go on, you bleeders, laugh, 'cos I know you're dying to!'

Well, they couldn't get door off her for laughing. Poor mam. She was only little, tinier than me and only ever had one eye.

She had an accident at home when she was seven and course in them days they couldn't afford to do anything and she never had a glass eye because they couldn't afford to buy her one.

She always said, 'When I were young, they all used to say, "Oh poor old Mary with all them bairns."' She says they all used to feel sorry for her, but she says 'I'm richer and happier than any of them that only had one and two.'

Every weekend it didn't matter whose house she went to, she was so welcome with her children 'cos we all loved her so much. And like she used to come here perhaps five weeks on trot, and then she'd say, 'I can't come next week, I'll have to go to our so-and-so's to keep cart on wheels.' So we didn't fall out. She had what we called a 'dossing bag' – it were a little shopping bag she used. If she were stopping two nights it were two pairs of pants, two vests, a clean top, and extra pair of trousers, depending on whose house she went to, because some of them went to pub at weekends like us and some of them didn't. It was true when she said they all pitied her, but she were richer than any of 'em. As she got older she had the loveliest life.

Mary had a big heart, and she would do what she could for others. For instance, one of her son's friends had found himself homeless after his wife threw him out; he asked if he could stay for a few days. Despite being badly overcrowded in the house already, Mary didn't hesitate in offering him a roof over his head. She told him to 'get in wi' lads'. He was there for three-and-a-half years; Denise says it was just like having another brother.

The house had the lads' bedroom, the parents' bedroom and the girls' room. When her father died, Denise says they got rid of the big bed and put three singles in that room.

Her mother must have cut an odd figure: a small, one-eyed woman, invariably with a cigarette in her mouth. But Mary was well known and loved in her community. Denise says that when Mary died the whole village of Brampton came to a standstill for the funeral. In his address the vicar said that Mary was not one for coming to services, but her home was like a church as it was open to all in need and God was there.

It was easy to spot Denise's house in Brampton – a pebble-dashed semi that had been extended at the back. Whenever I went past, the door was invariably open, even in winter. I had been there a number of times and there was always a lot of activity, with people coming and going or the phone ringing. There was a happy madness about the place.

Recently when I stopped off to see them, I found Denise and Barry struggling to get a frail old lady out of their car. The woman had a tuft of white hair, bottle-end glasses and few teeth, but she seemed happy enough as the pair manoeuvred her into their house. Denise explained that they had just taken the woman for a day out. She wasn't a relative, but Denise had been looking after her as she had been through a tough time. The woman's carer had sold the lady's house from under her feet and stolen all her money, so she was left with nothing. Then she had been badly treated by the medics.

When I said to the old lady that she was in good hands she gave me a gummy smile and a nod – she knew the cavalry had arrived. Denise gave the woman a hug and said they were going to have a 'beautifying evening' – she was going to do her hair and make-up to cheer her up. I am not sure if the old lady understood, but she seemed glad of any kindness that came her way. Denise was someone who would take charge and lend a hand to those worse off than herself. Just like her mum. Barry was her willing deputy. She was the captain without a doubt, and Barry was happy to be first mate. Barry did a lot of the running around for the community centre, ferrying supplies and people. He did grumble a bit, but he fell in line nonetheless. Inevitably, working at the centre meant there was less time to do the housework at home. It could have been a disaster if the men were not supportive. Denise says that, without Barry being 100 per cent behind her, she could not have done what she has over the years. He even did a lot of the cooking and childcare at home.

When Cortonwood Comeback first opened it provided meals five days a week. Denise and the other women spent hours baking and trying to produce good food at as low a cost as possible. I remember one of the women telling me that it was considered quite a gift being able to 'split a penny'. Years of poverty had taught the women how to get the most for the least.

Basically, I cooked and baked five days a week for centre and seven days a week at home; he used to do dinners at home. Honest to God, I've got to say this, if it weren't for Barry I couldn't have done a tenth of what I did, truly I couldn't. I've got to say that, its not all down to me. What I couldn't do in house if I didn't have time he did, and if I couldn't get here or I couldn't get there, and to this day he still does all the running up and down for community centre.

The venture became a way of life for the couple, with Barry just as involved as Denise.

We had mothers and toddlers, we had senior citizens, you name it and we had it. But gradually over the years what's happened what I said would happen, and it so gutted me because like everything went didn't it – there's more people living in this village now that I don't know than there is that I do. It's happened over last twenty years, because slowly but surely older end haven't gone but younger, they go; they don't go far but they've gone anyway. I'm lucky actually, sometimes I'm not so lucky 'cos sometimes it's a pain, but my five kids have all stayed near me – two lives in same street, two lives on

54

same road down there and one lives up road. I believe as well as a community thing it's a family thing isn't it? You are what your parents are because I'm what me mother were.

When we last spoke Denise was in the midst of a battle to stop the centre being made homeless, as the Methodists – a different group from the one that helped the centre get established twenty years ago – were trying to sell the building. She and Barry were part of a steering group to fight the move, or to figure out how to raise the £90,000 needed to buy the place. Keeping the centre open had always been a full-time occupation. There was a feeling that without the Fitzpatricks' determination it would disappear along with the community it was set up to help. It did have the feel of a place struggling to survive against the odds. You couldn't say this to Denise or Barry, though, as they were still as much involved as ever.

You can fight the system and those who run it, but you can't fight time. And that was one thing that Denise did not have a lot of. For over a decade she had been dealing with her own set of health problems. She had suffered numerous heart attacks, was a diabetic, and had asthma. She had been through major heart surgery – a quadruple bypass. Barry said she had had seven heart attacks, but Denise wasn't so sure; she had lost count. If the doctors were right she might not be around to see the twenty-fifth anniversary of the strike. But true to form, Denise had other plans. She had a favourite grandchild called Lucy, who was seven, and she was determined to be around long enough to see her grow up.

I don't know how many bloody heart attacks I've had. It's three years since I had massive heart attack and they said it's congenital heart disease. Well a lot of me mam's family just dropped down dead and a lot of my family have, me brothers; apart from me sister Bettie, none of mine have reached sixty-two, so when I'm sixty-two I'm having a party. I were told it would be a very, very brave man who undertook to do a transplant, and in any case they said I couldn't have one because I were diabetic and asthmatic; the medication I take weren't compatible with anti-rejection drugs you have to take for rest of your life. So I says to doctor 'What do I do then?' She says, 'There isn't a lot you can do, Denise'.

It's a few years since I've had a really, really serious illness. I've never been poorly in me life, and I don't want you to think I'm saying that, because I haven't been ill. I've had heart attacks and I've had heart surgery, but as soon as they've got you and they've brought you round, you're not what I would call ill. You're a bit weak, but you come round and you're not physically ill. I had heart surgery and I'll tell you something, I went in, and I'm not just saying it, but to me it were like holiday and I were coming out a new person, and I did. I were back at work in seven weeks. I were cleaning, I were supervisor. Only thing I didn't do were mopping and hoovering, but I used to dust, I used to polish, I used to wash down.

I've done everything I wanted to do – I can say that in all honesty. If anything happens to me, the only thing that bothers me – apart from Barry; he'll look after himself – not even me children, me grandchildren, but if I can see Lucy get to sixteen I will be very, very, happy.

Denise cut her campaigning teeth when she worked at a car-battery factory. She says she didn't look for a trade union role, it was foisted upon her by male colleagues who were worried about how the company would react if it were known they had set up a union on the premises. They 'volunteered' Denise as their representative and then they gradually dropped out of the union, leaving her and a group of the other women to fight for the right to maintain a union.

Before that I were militant to point I always fought for underdog; in fact when I went to work if anybody wanted owt they'd say go and ask Denise. Then when men formed a union they were the most spineless set of men I've ever come across in all my life.

It were Transport and General, and it were when we worked at battery factory and conditions were terrible, and I mean terrible. One of lasses – a lovely girl, Sandra Sloane – she weren't a bit bolshy or owt, and she walked past me this day, she says, 'Alright sister!' And each time she went past, she said 'Alright sister,' so when we got in to have our lunch break, 'What's up with you?', she says. 'You never told me that there were a union and you were in it', I says.

'I'm not in union – I didn't even know there were a bloody union', she says.

'There is,' I says. 'Who's told you?', she says. 'Alf . . .' I said. 'I don't believe him', she says. 'He showed me card, they're all in union, but they daren't tell boss, you see', I says. 'The swines!'

Anyway, it finished up we all joined union didn't we, and really they do educate yer – they do; about meetings and so on. Finished up they needed a shop steward, so guess who got shop steward's job? The men daren't do it. They dropped out one by one.

At that time Denise was working on a production line making batteries for Mini and Rover cars at a firm called Jones' Batteries, which has long since ceased to exist. They were the big car batteries with seven and nine plates of lead in them, respectively. It was dangerous work as the staff were handling lead and acid. According to Denise the safety standards were appalling. The firm did not provide the staff with rubber gloves; they had to bring their own, and so people didn't bother. The question of lead poisoning was not discussed.

There were fans above the work stations to disperse the poisonous fumes, but Denise says they never worked. There weren't even proper toilet facilities.

There'd be twelve to thirteen women, and all we had were a toilet up yard. There were no sanitary towel machines, nothing of any sort of hygiene, and when you went for your snack you had a sink and two electric kettles. I mean that were progress – electric kettles; you made your cups of tea and you sat, and you had to wash your hands in this sink, and you sat in this little room and had your sandwiches, never knowing really how much danger you were in from lead.

I mean I used to wear gloves, because it used to splash me fingers, not because it were owt to do with me getting lead poisoning. We had fans over our machines; they never chuffing worked, they just looked like fans, you know what I mean.

It is easy to see why the arrival of the Transport and General Workers Union in this workplace was not welcomed by the owner. The boss, Ron Jones, was dead against a union. The staff were too scared to hold meetings anywhere near the plant for fear he might find out. Inevitably, he had it in for Denise, who was the union representative and had a reputation as a trouble-maker. She says he was a tyrant who would have a go at her each day, hoping she would step out of line so she could be sacked. But she managed to keep her temper, only just.

He'd like goad me and goad me 'cos he wanted to sack me, and he couldn't sack me for nowt, could he? Every day, before I even got into factory, he'd be waiting at doors and I'd be walking down to clock on, and he'd be saying this and that and the other to me. I used to totally ignore him, then every so often I think, God if he starts this morning he's mine, you know. And we'd have these matches; literally, if ever one of us had struck first blow we'd have killed each other. Were bloody awful. Anyway, he sold out to this big firm Armstrongs, but he kept on as general manager.

Anyway, there were an assistant, and this man, he were lovely. He asked us into office to talk to us all. He says to me, 'I've heard you're a trouble-causer.' I says 'No I'm not.' I says, 'If going in and asking for a sanitary towel dispenser for women is causing trouble, well then yeah, if asking for an incinerator is causing trouble, then yeah I am. Or if asking for rubber gloves to be provided instead of us having to buy our own, three or four pair a week, you'd have a new pair every day, then if that is causing trouble then you're right, I am.' I said all these things, and he says 'I'll take your word for it, 'cos you're not like I've been led to believe,' and I says to him, 'Well I'm not.'

The chance to get rid of Denise came when the company decided to discontinue the line of batteries that she had been making. But she didn't go without a fight.

When he discontinued line, and batteries I were making were for Minis and Rovers, we went to unfair dismissal; and I'm not kidding, that man, every time we won, he appealed. But we still finished up with money, and only thing we didn't get was us job back, and there were no way would he reinstate us, and that's what we wanted from day one. Anyway, I got about £2,700 didn't I? It were a bloody fortune, we bought us caravan with it, didn't we?

Denise got her first real experience of being on a demonstration when she went to support the steelworkers in London in the late seventies. She was thirty-three, and from that moment there was no turning back; she had found her *métier*.

We went on a rally and I had this banner made – well, it were a placard – and it were a picture of Maggie Thatcher. June Bailey, who painted it, could do fabulous characters – you know, she can do characters and cartoons and things, and she did it and it were Maggie Thatcher with blonde hair, great big teeth, and a knife dripping blood, and where it were cut through it said, 'Make the last cut – Maggie's throat'. And do you know what I did? I got on the front page of *Socialist Worker*, and in colour, and then in another paper.

We walked all the way through London, and that's when I heard all songs like 'Oh Maggie Thatcher's got one, Norman Tebbit is one . . .' That were when I got a taste for it, because we were all in same situation.

She did get a bit carried away, though, and brought the placard in to work at the battery factory before the march in London. She thought she wasn't likely to get caught as the boss was away that day. But a not-so-loyal colleague told him later that she had been playing the fool, chanting and waving the banner around at her work-station. He had a go at her, but luckily that was all he could do, as he had no real proof that she had broken company regulations. And none of Denise's other workmates was going to say anything.

I mean, we were so solid, those of us that were left in union. Anyway, I took plaque to work 'cos Ron, the boss, he had a big yacht, and it used to be in Med. Anyway, he fetched it up north and it were at Whitby, so every Friday morning he used to sod off and come back Monday afternoon, or Monday dinner-time.

So Thursday when I got this banner I took it to work, didn't I, to show 'em what I were going to London with. Trudy Simpson, she got it out, and I can honestly say I never marched. I never shifted from my grid, 'cos I daren't, for simple reason if I moved it's a black strike against you. I didn't smoke so I didn't have to go toilets for a fag, so I stood at my grid. There were no way I would do anything that he could sack me for.

So Trudy, she gets this placard and she's marching round, and all my mates up at line were marching round and they were shouting, 'Maggie, Maggie, Maggie, out, out, out'. Honestly, we were hysterical, even them that weren't in union. Everybody were laughing, men come out to have a look, so it finished up men and women walking round factory; that were on Friday morning. God, Monday morning, when I got into work and he were waiting at door, 'You!' I says, 'What?' He says, 'I'm telling you now you're up that yard.' I says, 'Why, what have I done?' He says, 'For bringing your politics into work.' I says, 'I didn't bring no politics into work.'

I'm stood nose-to-nose to him. He says, 'You did, and you were walking round factory.' I says 'I never, ever walked round the factory with anything,' I says, 'I didn't even join in march.' I says, 'there were only me at me grid.' So he couldn't get me down with that.

Denise is a bit like a bright light to moths; she attracts people around her and things seem to happen when she is about. She is never happier than when she is speaking her mind. People who tried to get the better of her often found themselves the butt of a joke. On one trip down to London, for a march during the 1984/85 strike, the police kept pulling their coach over.

Police kept stopping us every few yards when we were nearing London, and this copper comes onto bus. I says, 'When he gets on, leave it to me.' So anyway, he stood on bus and he says, 'What they call yer?' I says, 'Denise Fitzpatrick.' 'Where are you from?' I told him. He says, 'So you're going to thing?' I says, 'No we're not, not today we're not.' He says, 'Why not today?' I says, 'We're so hard-up.' I said to him – this is the truth – 'we're so hard-up and these women have been prostituting themselves, and today I've told 'em there'll be plenty of people there and we're going on bus today, and all that they earn they keep theirselves,' it's true.

And nobody on bus said a word, and he just says 'You're a smart cow, aren't you?' I says, 'You can call me anything, but don't call me a cow. If my husband knows you've called me a cow, honest to God, he would genuinely, really kill you.' You didn't call people animals, swines, dogs, pigs, never. Well, we did coppers and that, but not proper people.

Denise says she was often targeted in a crowd, perhaps because her white hair made her stand out or because she was more bolshy than most. She decided to buy a wig to wear at marches, so the police wouldn't spot her so easily. After months of demonstrating, she was becoming sick of the abuse. She says the police would shout, 'Get that white-haired bitch!', and call the women whores, spitting at them. I am sure the women gave as good as they got, and they say the abuse fired them up rather than intimidated them. Denise got a letter from some soldiers during the dispute that was addressed to 'The thing with white hair'. Even today, she cannot bring herself to repeat the foul language it contained. But rather than discouraging her, it gave Denise encouragement; she decided that if people could sink so low, then they were the sick and twisted ones; the way she saw it she was fighting for families, jobs and the community, whereas they were just disgusting and had taken the fight onto a personal level. Certainly, she wasn't a woman you would forget, as the leader of one of Britain's biggest unions discovered when, by chance, he spent the day in her company.

We went on this demonstration in London, and it were a glorious day. Police actually put a line up and they stopped the rally getting into Hyde Park, so I don't know where we were, which part we were in.

Anyway, we were in this square and we didn't have money. You know it were a fallacy though, that no one had money – a lot of them did. I don't know where they got it from, but we never did, and we used to pool what we had. We'd take our sandwiches, take us drinks, and it was absolutely red hot – there was about six of us, same ones that went to all rallies, and it were like a carnival, and we didn't have no money between us. There were this pub, and people were coming out with pints.

I says, 'Look, we'll put together and I'll go and fetch a pint of shandy, and we'll have to share it between us.' I goes to bar; by the time I got to front I had two quid, 'cos we knew it were dear in London, and I got this pint of shandy. He said something, £2, so I gave him £2, and he were saying something to me, and I'm stood waiting on change, and he's waiting on me giving him some more money, and it were about £2.10p.

I says, 'I ain't got no more money – £2.10p for a chuffing pint!' And this fellow at side of me, he says, 'What's up love?' I says '£2.10p for a pint of shandy, and to cap it all there's six of us to share it when we get out!' I says, 'I ain't got 10p,' and this feller, he were rolling with laughing. I says to him, 'Honest to God, you can come back with me, we're not flash and full of money. I've got two lads on strike as well as me husband, there's no chuffing money to get boozed up.' Well this fella, he says 'That's your 10p, and give her another five pints.'

I says, 'I can't carry five more pints!' and pub were chokka. He shouted these two blokes over, we all went out, and we all had this pint of shandy. Anyway, we finished up we were talking, honest to God, laughing and talking all time – I hadn't a clue who he were. We finished up sat down. Christine, my mate, she were big, bigger than me, and she were raw all between her legs. It were like liver, she couldn't walk for over a

63

week, 'cos it were that hot and her legs were rubbing. Anyway, we finished up sat on pavement and these fellas sat down with us and we were talking, and they kept calling each other names – another one called Eric and this one were Ray. Anyway, when we finally got moving, it were time to go back to chuffing buses – they wouldn't let us get to rally.

As we're going, this fella he says to me, 'Well I've had a lovely day in your company', he says, 'and you haven't a clue who you've been with all day, have you?' I says, 'No' and when it were time to go, he bought us all another drink to walk back to bus with, and he says, 'Well, I'm Ray Buckton' [then leader of the powerful train-driver's union, ASLEF]. I says 'You never chuffing are!' He says, 'I am, honestly.' I says, 'well, I'd have never believed it!'

That were on Sunday. Then on Friday night I'm up at club at bingo, 'cos I used to run bingo – I used to run bleeding everything. But anyway, and I tell you one of the fellas came in; he says, 'Denise, there's a bloody railway van outside your house, I've told him there's nobody in and he says, "Does Denise Fitzpatrick live in?" And I says I'd send you down.'

So I come down, and I says 'What's up?' He says, 'I've got you some stuff.' Well you've never seen owt like it in your life. There were giant tins of catering soup. They were massive, not just your ordinary catering; they must have bought them for bloody railway, 'cos they were this big [arms open wide], and there were coffee, sugar, soup, all things that you just put water in. You should have seen it. And there were about five of these boxes, and then at front there were one and it said, 'Personal: Denise Fitzpatrick.' Driver, he says 'This has been put on last and this hasn't got to go to strike centre, this is to come to your house.' So I says, 'What is it?' He says, 'I don't know, I honestly don't know.'

Anyway, we brought it down, and honest, it were full. During strike it were like a soup kitchen in my house, as we had mass pickets, everything, and everybody came here and I used to make soup and that for 'em. It were from Ray Buckton's wife Barbara; she said like it were for what I used in my house, because everybody used to come.

Denise saw Ray again at the Miners' Gala in 1985, when he was a guest speaker. He made a point of tracking her down and introducing his wife.

As I said earlier, one of Denise's saving graces is that she has the ability to laugh off most of life's tribulations, although at the time she doesn't always see the funny side of things. She says she lost the plot once, eight months into the strike. As usual, she was rushing around trying to please everyone, doing the housework and a job to bring in some money. It was tough, as she had a husband and two sons on strike. This is an extract from a charity book the women at the Comeback published in 1994, called *Ten Years on and Still Laughing*.

It was late November and no signs of them going back to work; with two kids still at school things looked bleak. I had done my early morning shift and the men were picketing at the docks. They had been out since about three a.m. When they got home I was preparing the dinner. Mince, peas, carrots and mashed potatoes. As they took their boots off it was 'Mam, put t' kettle on', 'Mam hurry up wit' dinner,' 'Denise, I'm starving.'

By this time it was quarter-to-four, and I had to catch the half-past-four bus to work. None of them had read the signs that I was ready to explode; they trooped into other room and left me to mash the potatoes, set the table and dish out the dinner, which I admit was unusual, as Barry usually helped out. I shouted and asked if someone would come and set the table. All three must have had earplugs in, as the only response was silence and no one stirred. By this time I was so annoyed I emptied the pan of potatoes into the middle of the table, spread them out and poured on the carrots, peas, and last but not least the mince. I got my coat on and stood in doorway and said calmly, 'Dinner's on table.' I fairly ran to bus stop so they couldn't drag me back to clean up mess.

After work Barry arrived in old van he used for picketing and never said a word. When we got home our Robert said 'Mam, next time we have mince, put a crust on it and there won't be as much mess.' With that we all howled with laughter, and things were back to normal.

Out of the destruction of the pits Denise went on to carve out a role for herself in Brampton. She told me that when the strike began, she made a vow that the miners would not be beaten and, although they lost the fight for jobs she felt they had won on other levels; they had gained from their loss. They had found friendship and solidarity among thousands of people, inside and outside of the mining communities. Many of those who developed lifelong friendships during the strike were strangers or just on nodding terms before.

Denise and those around her decided they weren't going to go into oblivion. She says they realised they were capable of doing things, and she admitted they needed something for themselves as well as for the community. They had been active for so long they found they couldn't wind down. She feels the years of hard work have not been wasted, and she is 'proud fit to bust' of what they have achieved.

Denise was brought up in a large family unit, where poverty was a way of life and everyone mucked in together and shared what they had. The world revolved around her mother, and it is that legacy that she has passed on to those around her – in particular, her children.

The logo for the Comeback centre is 'Tall Oaks from Little Acorns Grow', a saying that could equally well be applied to the women who became involved in supporting the strike. For

Denise, the seeds of this were planted in her childhood; she was brought up to make the best of things. Despite the poverty, she has never wanted for much in her life. I did ask her what her ambition had been when she was young. She said the only thing that she had ever really longed for was her own dressing-table. Being brought up in a packed house meant there was no room or money for such a luxury. At this, Barry protested and pointed out that he had got her one years ago. Denise laughed. What she was trying to say was that she had been fortunate, as her material needs had mostly been met and she had been blessed with a loving family. Denise had achieved a lot for a woman whose only ambition in life was to own a dressing-table.

CHAPTER THREE

Not So Dumb After All:
Betty Cook

Betty Cook was a woman after my own heart. I realised this when she told me one of the worst things that happened to her during the strike wasn't having her knee broken by a police truncheon – although that was fairly nasty – but having a new pair of sexy red boots destroyed in the skirmishes. Twenty years on, her knee was better but she still pined for her late-lamented footwear. I could totally sympathise with her, as I had lost many a beloved pair of shoes in the line of duty.

We were only supposed to be chatting for a couple of hours; I promised her it wouldn't take any longer. She is one of those busy people who always have a full diary and a million things to do. But I'm afraid I broke my promise, and in the end I was with Betty for most of the day.

To steal some words from Queen Elizabeth I, Betty might have the body of a frail and feeble woman, but inside she had the heart and stomach of a king. Betty had become a people's champion. The skills she had gained as a result of the 1984/5 strike gave her the confidence and insight to build a whole new life.

These days she is often asked to speak at colleges and meetings about the role of women. This isn't because she is a proponent of women's liberation, though; it is because in Betty you have the real thing: a woman who has gone from being a downtrodden housewife with little education or ambition to a university graduate and respected public speaker. It didn't happen overnight; Betty has worked hard to dig herself out of the hole in which fate dropped her by way of birth.

The day we met up didn't start out brilliantly, as I couldn't find Betty's house. She hadn't actually given me a street name or house number. Her directions on the phone were given in the way that people who live in tiny country communities tend to give them – not bothering with precise detail. It's as if they feel that you simply *must* know where a place is, as though the information was so firmly ingrained in their minds that it would communicate itself to yours as if by telepathy. It's a case of 'You just go down there a bit, then turn a little left, a touch right and you can't miss it', all said in a voice that implies you would be an utter fool if you couldn't follow those directions.

Betty's home was in the village of Lower Pilley, near Barnsley. I was to drive past a small primary school, down a country lane beyond a discount store, and it would be there after a few semis. It was part of a terrace and I couldn't miss it. I think Betty's navigational skills must have been far superior to mine as, no matter how I zoomed up and down the single-track roads, upsetting cyclists and walkers alike, I couldn't spot the place. In the end I had to resort to the mobile and a plea of being a bit lost. You wouldn't think that I had successfully managed to navigate myself around war zones. Betty came to the end of her road and waved me towards the pretty row of terraced houses that had been winking at me each time I passed. Fortunately she didn't seem to mind that I was tardy and in a fluster – I can't stand being late for anything.

The terrace was built in hefty stone blocks that had blackened over time. You see rows of houses like this dotted all over Yorkshire. Once upon a time they were regarded as humble homes. Today they are considered to be cute and trendy. Their value has therefore increased dramatically. The house at the end of Betty's terrace that needed complete gutting was selling for just under £100,000. For an uninhabitable two-up two-down, that is the kind of sum that produces wolf-whistles in these parts. There was plenty of open countryside nearby, but I thought it was marred a bit by the deep grumble of the nearby M1. But no one minded; in Yorkshire, being close to a major road network was considered a bonus, and bugger the noise.

Betty had rented her place for years, and she had warned me that she was no domestic goddess. She said her home was a bit like something out of the TV programme *Steptoe and Son*: full of bits and pieces. Apparently, her three cats had things firmly under their control. In reality her home was comfortable, with lots of mementoes and photos. Although she was right about her cats – they did rule the roost, especially the big tomcat who tried to eat my tape recorder and then went for one of the female cats. I was to learn that, as the only male in the house these days, he had some big boots to fill.

When you step into Betty's home you also step into her world. As you get cosy in her easy chair and stroke the cats, sipping sweet tea, you find yourself suspending your own reality in order to listen to hers. I'd been looking forward to meeting Betty; I had read about her and recalled her from the strike twenty years ago. She was a prominent figure in WAPC. Betty was the epitome of the kind of woman I wanted to include in this book. The *Guardian* did a piece about her to mark the twentieth anniversary of the dispute. In it she spoke of how she had thought she had been stupid when she was much younger – the daughter, wife and mother of miners – but all that changed in those twelve months. I didn't see her as a working-class hero; like all the women I spoke to, she was dead against being categorised in that way. They felt that their actions came out of necessity. I recognised that they were not 'superwomen'; if they ever wore their pants over their tights it was more to do with absentmindedness than superhero status.

The strike did change their lives, but in most cases it served to bring out what was already there. If a marriage was unhappy, then it didn't survive; the cracks grew wider as the pressure became greater. Whereas the strong relationships – whether it was within couples or among friends – got stronger. They stood the test of time, hardship acting as a bond. Prior to the strike many of the women in these communities had been rigidly controlled by their families and by the strict traditions they were born into. The resentment inevitably came to the fore when they found a voice. For some, their natural intelligence was overlooked or put down as a freak of nature, and therefore ignored or frowned upon. But once the women's eyes and mouths were opened it was a case of 'having lit the touch paper, stand well back'.

Betty was a firecracker still fizzing and popping all these years on. When you first met her there was nothing in Betty's manner that betrayed the passion and anger that lay within. She didn't rant and rave; there was no steam coming from her ears nor froth at her mouth. I knew by repute that she did have it in her to vent her rage, but that was in hostile environments where she was fighting a cause. Here in her comfy living room, circled by her cats, she exuded warmth. Betty came across as a personable and kind-hearted soul. Perhaps the first giveaway as to what lay beneath was the T-shirt she was wearing. It declared, '1984–2004: I'd still rather be a picket than a scab.' It was made for a twentieth-anniversary celebration held by WAPC in October 2004.

The second giveaway came as I sat her down and talked to her in detail about her life. A deep-rooted anger manifested itself. It was hidden below the surface, but it was there alright. To understand her you need to understand what happened to mould her into who she is today. It was her ability to turn the power of her anger into a tool to help herself and her children survive that got her through life's injustices. Betty, known as

Cookie to many, is about 5ft 1in, and compact in every way. She was sixty-six when we met in the autumn of 2004, but her spiky blondish-grey hair and clear skin made her look much younger. She had the air of someone who had been there, done it, got the T-shirt – quite a few T-shirts actually – and was more than happy to pass on the wisdom gleaned. But she was just as happy to admit that, despite her many years on the front line, she still had a lot to learn. As she said herself, the decades of skirmishes, both mental and physical, had not robbed her of a certain naivety; perhaps that was what kept her from becoming too hardened by her lot.

Betty was small, but solid as a rock – like the song the women were so fond of singing. She's what I would call an old-fashioned socialist. When I was a young reporter in Yorkshire, I used to come across them all the time; these days they are as rare as pithead baths. She was the kind of socialist who had more to do with Robin Hood than Dom Perignon. Betty's life had been dominated by the coal industry. Both sides of her family worked in the pits; her paternal grandfather helped sink the shaft at Frickley colliery. She married a miner whose family had a similar background. His father had been killed in an underground accident several years before Betty's children were born. Her father died only two years after retiring, having spent his whole working life in a coal mine. Two of her three sons went into the industry.

Mining was in Betty's blood, bred into her as a way of life. Part of that social programming was to influence what she felt she could achieve in her life. The women were not brought up to have ambition beyond the home. The men toiled in the pits, while wives and mothers laboured in the kitchen or with the children. It was not questioned, it was simply how things were. Women's liberation was something to do with la-di-da folks down south – only the middle classes could afford the time and cost of burning bras.

Betty laughs now as she remembers that, when she was younger, she'd heard of the movement and thought women really were burning articles of clothing all over the place, and imagined bonfires of Playtex bras. She didn't recognise it was mostly a metaphor until many years later. She didn't really understand what women's lib was. When a male reporter asked her during the 1984/5 strike if she was a 'libber', she replied 'If you tell me what that is then I might be able to answer you.'

Her 'liberation' had nothing to do with lofty academia; she'd never read *The Female Eunuch*. For the likes of Betty, the reality was as basic as it got – new-found freedoms were an unexpected spin-off in the fight for survival. In a tough world you learned how to be hard, and utilise what skills you had to get through the worst times. As with many coalfield women, the strike 'mobilised' her, in the same way that the Second World War changed women's roles and freed them from the kitchen – women took on male roles, in jobs like welding, farming and running essential services.

In Britain's strike-bound coalfields in 1984/5, women mirrored the role of their men – they became flying pickets and activists. They stood alongside the miners, they were among the casualties in clashes with police. For the first time in their lives they truly shared the hardships of their men. As women were not allowed down pits to work, they didn't know first hand what it was like to labour in those conditions. But when the strike began they found that they could be with the men to face the danger, determination and eventual despair of the picket lines. In fact, it was the women who often caused the biggest headaches for the police. One officer told me that they would rather deal with thirty male pickets than ten women, as the latter were so unpredictable and hard to handle.

At the same time, though, they were doing more than the men – they were nurturing those involved in the dispute. They transformed their traditional role by broadening their family group to the whole community. The women continued to do their usual work – bringing up the kids, washing, cooking and cleaning, and part-time jobs – but added to this picketing, fund-raising, attending political rallies and running soup kitchens. Tiring it might have been, but it was truly a labour of love.

Betty was working a 20-hour day. She would pop home just to change and for a quick bite to eat, and then she would be out again. Her mother worried about the state of the house, but Betty joked that the cobwebs would be useful at Christmas, as they could be sprayed with silver paint and decorated. There is no doubt that Betty loved every minute of it; even when she was badly injured her new-found spirit drove her on.

The strike was an education; the women learned more about politics in those twelve months than could ever have been achieved by years at a college or university.

Betty described herself as a doormat prior to the strike. Her husband, Donald, would come and go as he pleased. He was the archetypal miner. At work in the pit all day, he would come home, expect his dinner on the table, wash and change, then go to the pub. It was a daily routine; it left Betty alone and scared. She was only 18, and pregnant, when she married; he was 23. She'd gone out with Donald on the rebound from another romance but, as she says, 'When you got pregnant in those days, you married, and that was that.'

She stayed married for more than thirty years. She describes it as an unhappy marriage, but she clung on to the tradition and the institution for her children. She waited for her time to come, which it did. Betty assiduously learned from her world of hardship and hate. Each tear she shed – and there were many – would add to her resolve. Donald, in her view, was a bad husband. He showed no love or care. She says that some weeks he would give her housekeeping money, other weeks he would spend it all in the pub. Turning the clock back to the strike of 1972, Betty has vivid memories of feeling helpless, useless, thick and stupid, isolated and paralysed with her own ignorance, and kept firmly under control by her bullying husband.

These days it is hard to imagine the degree of poverty that was considered the norm for many mining families. When Betty and Donald married, they didn't have a home of their own.

We lived with his aunt and uncle at first, at Staincross, and then when Michael was about twelve months we got this so-called pithouse that was on Woolley Edge, near Woolley pit. It was very isolated: no bus, no shop, no nothing really, apart from a telephone box. They were really, really old cottages. There were back-to-back houses and a few council houses that they had built. It was on a hill, and Woolley colliery was at the bottom.

They called it Brick Row – if I ever write my life story it will be called *The Road From Brick Row*. It was awful. The people there were so horrible; they all intermarried so you didn't know who was related to who. I was totally an outsider. I was known as the 'comer-in'. They made life hell for me. There were outside toilets and most of them were shared, but we had our own and the children would walk past one woman's toilet to go and play in the field. She would come and complain about them walking that way, and say nasty things. At that time I wasn't strong; I used to bring the children in, then I'd hide away and cry and cry. In those days if I went in a shop and they short-changed me I wouldn't dare say anything.

Betty had come from a good home. She was an only child, and her parents were loving, but they were staunchly traditional. This meant that once Betty was married and a mother herself, then she was expected to stand on her own two feet and make the best of things. They weren't cruel, but they were strict. So Betty had come from a comfortable house with hot and cold running water and an indoor toilet to the bleak world of 'Brick Row', a ghetto on the front line of poverty, where some days there was no running water at all and the properties were infested with rats.

Young and scared, she didn't feel she had anyone to turn to; her neighbours continued to treat her like an outsider. But this young mum could only be pushed so far. She recalls the moment when in her own words she 'began to turn'.

I turned before the strike in the seventies. This particular day I was so unhappy. All my husband did was live in the pub, so we weren't a family. I felt there was just me and the boys, really isolated from everything.

Because we were isolated we used to get mobile butcher van, the mobile Co-op and bakery. Our Michael used to spend a lot of time at my mum's before he went to school, so he was with her that day. I went to the butcher van this one morning, and this neighbour who had been really horrible in the past said, 'It's not fair what your Michael has been doing this morning,' and I said, 'No, Michael has not been doing anything this morning,' and the woman said, 'Oh yes he has, he has been tormenting the Kelsey children.' So I said, 'No, it wasn't Michael. Was it Donny?' Although there was seventeen months between them, they did look alike. And she said, 'I know the bloody difference between your boys.' That were it. I just blew, and the butcher just stood with his mouth open. I said, 'Well he's done bloody well to get over here when he's with my mother at South Elmsall.' I blew a fuse. I said, 'Get out of this van now before that goes straight in your face [at this point she was waving her fist and scrunching up her face to look menacing], and she ran.' And I just grabbed my stuff and I went in to the house and I shook. I couldn't believe what I had done. That was the first time I had blown. I was in my early twenties. But I had had enough of them.

The house was a little two-up, two-down, no hot water, no bathroom, outside loo – and I had been used to the creature comforts. We had this cellar and my ex wouldn't put a light in this cellar, and it was really dark and horrible, and of course the coal was in the cellar, so some nights I was too scared to go down there; I would have to sit cold. At the beginning all we had was a table and straight chairs; we didn't have an easy chair. I was so lonely and so unhappy, and because my parents were of the old type – 'You have made your bed, now you lie on it' – so I couldn't go and talk to mum. Everything was building up.

My mother-in-law was so horrid to me; whatever my ex did she stuck up for him and it was my fault. It was a case of 'If he didn't give us any money then it was up to him, as he earned it so he could decide what to do with it'. Some weeks he didn't give us any money. I used to go to mum's every other weekend with the boys, and mum always packed me up with a bag of food to come home with, and every week there was a letter from mum with a ten-shilling note in, and in those days ten shillings went a long way. I didn't tell my ex about it.

He had three aunties who were quite good to me, and some days they would take the kids and I used to say, 'I'm not bothered about myself but would you feed the children for me?' At one stage we lived on mashed potatoes and beef broth. I couldn't face it now, I feel sick even thinking about it. For clothes, mum was very good. She used to knit and buy the boys things. She was the old-fashioned type – to show love was to knit. I could never have talked to her and sat down and said, 'Mum, I am so unhappy, this and that has happened.'

From that moment in the butcher's van when she threatened to punch one of her neighbours, Betty discovered a new strength.

It was a facet of her character that she was to develop over the years. She realised that if she made a fuss things would happen; it was a case of 'squeaky wheels'. So when her water supply was virtually cut off in the daytime because it was being used at the local pit for a new machine that washed coal, this time she wasn't just going to hide in the house and cry about it.

When the colliery got this new washer there was an agreement that they would only draw water for it during the night, as the water pressure where we lived was not very good. But they didn't stick to that, and some days we had no water at all. I got so incensed that I took my two boys to Wakefield Social Services, and sat them on the desk and said, 'These kids are dirty; they have no clean cups, saucers, plates. You sort it out because I am not.'

This was me starting to come out, but only because of the kids. They said, 'You can't just abandon your kids', and I said, 'You just try me.' So they said, 'If you promise to take your kids home we will make phone calls and get something done.' One was only a baby, so to make bottles I used to have to put both kids in pram, walk down to mother-in-law's with pot bottles. I'd fill them with water and come back again. Sometimes when I made the baby's bottle there was no water to cool it, so I used to have to stand outside and was there waving this bottle about for ages.

Then this guy from Woolley Edge Colliery came up our street – the pit was just at the bottom of the hill. He shouted, 'Who is this bloody woman who can't wash her bloody kids and make her baby's bottles?' I said it was me, and that he'd better get it sorted out. But they didn't. We still had a problem with the water for some time. When Donny no longer needed a bottle, this woman with a baby came up to me and said, 'What are you going to do about this water situation? I have no water to make my bottles.' I said, 'You do it, you see to it yourself.' I wasn't having anything to do with it; nobody helped me, so on yer bike.

And then I got rats in the cellar, and all the old ones said to me was that while you've got rats you've not got mice. I had to start again then. We were miles away from Wakefield, but that was our local authority so every time anything went wrong we were trying to liaise with Wakefield Council, and they didn't want to know – they didn't want us in the first place.

In the end I just wrote and said that I was going to take my two boys for medical examinations, and if they were suffering from anything that could possibly be put down to rats, then I would make the council suffer for it.

Conditions in the house were primitive. Betty's Brick Row was demolished in the 1980s, but she had a clear memory of what it was like. It's hard to imagine what a nightmare simple household chores were just forty-odd years ago. No central heating, no machines to help with the jobs. And rats in the cellar with young children in the house. Betty won the day. The council sent out a vermin control man to get rid of the rats, but the old women were right – as soon as they had gone, Betty had mice to contend with. Still, it was the lesser of two evils.

Being a miner's wife at that time wasn't a very happy experience. We had a set-pot in the corner in the kitchen. Do you know what that is? It was like a big iron cauldron, and underneath there is a little fire grate, and that's where you got your hot water from when you washed. You filled your set-pot with water, lit a fire underneath and it eventually warmed the water for washing and boiling your clothes. In those days you washed your clothes, you boiled them, you starched 'em, you blued 'em – you know what I mean? I had two peggy tubs, a little mangle and what you call a posser, which you used to churn 'em about.

I used to poss 'em about in the tub, through the mangle into another tub to rinse them, then into the set-pot for boiling, and then into the sink for another rinse and starching and what have you. Wash-day was horrendous. And when people talk today, and you say you didn't have a washing machine, you had this peggy tub, they don't believe you. This was only forty-six years ago. Donny suffered a lot with bronchitis, then Michael developed his epilepsy. Health visitors and everybody decided that the first council house that became empty, we would have to be rehoused, because of the children's health.

A council house did come empty on the estate nearby, but the local councillor lived at Woolley colliery, and he decided that he needed to move up to Windhill and I could have his house. So I told him what to do with it, as this was a better house away from the dirt of the colliery. I said, 'I am told that they are going to build some more houses and I am going to wait till then.' They did build the new council houses, and we got one. We had a bathroom – a toilet and hot water, it was like being on holiday. Prior to then, going to mum's once a fortnight, I had a bath at mum's and then it was a tin bath in front of the fire. Now we had a bathroom, and it was brilliant.

But the changes in Betty's life were only just beginning. When she was at school her mother had great ambitions for her – even her headmistress had insisted that she should carry on her studies and become a teacher. Betty wanted to be a nurse, but none of this was to be – marriage and having babies got in the way of that. The need to earn some money became more and more acute, as she was never certain where the next meal for the children was coming from. Relying on her husband was a poor option. Then an opportunity presented itself that opened the way for her first proper job, but only after placating her husband, who believed a wife shouldn't work.

By the time we moved to new house, I had Glyn so we had three boys. When Glyn was about 3½ a friend said to me they were wanting temporary staff for Christmas for Empire Stores, a mail-order company. She said if you want to go and work there I will look after Glyn for you. My ex-husband said no, you are not going out to work, blah blah. Eventually I said, well, if I pay the rent can I go? So he agreed that, yes, I could go. And I worked there that Christmas in the warehouse, and then they asked me if I wanted to go and work in the offices on a permanent basis. It is now the La Redoute group.

And the friend said she was perfectly happy looking after Glyn, so off I went to work. But then you had to work full-time and take holidays a week-block at a time. And even today I feel so guilty that I did work, because the boys didn't get all the attention that they should have got, particularly Glyn. And then the friend decided she didn't want to look after him any more. We had an arrangement because when she worked I looked after her daughter, so what we did, we paid each other's children's dinner monies.

Then mum looked after Glyn for a while, then a friend, and then he went to school. But I still feel very bad about it.

We got to '72 and my husband was a flying picket. I still worked, but we were cold; we didn't have coal and it was a long cold winter. We were also hungry, and I just cried the whole of the time. I was coming home from work trying to feed the boys while he was away flying picketing. He might come home just to pick up a change of clothes, and then off he would go again.

Social Services, DHSS as it was, wouldn't pay for the children because they said he was earning on the picket line, which he wasn't. By this time I had got more confidence, so I was writing letters. They kept saying they hadn't got the letters, and something told me to photocopy everything I sent, and in the end my husband went to a tribunal in Barnsley and the chair was very sympathetic. He said to my ex, 'How did you get here today, did you come by taxi?' And he said, 'No, I didn't even have the bus fare. I have had to walk.' And the judge went through all the stuff that I had sent. He said to the social, 'You pay him that money whatever you owe him, you give him his bus fare home, and you give him some money for food.' That was quite good, because we won that one. Well, I won that, because I had done all the letters and so on.

I was a different woman, but still nothing like how I changed in 1984/5. I still didn't have a lot of confidence; I was still like a doormat in the home. No difference in the home – I was working full-time, then coming home having to cook, wash, clean, iron, prepare meals for the next day. In an added role, trying to combine that with work, because my ex did nothing; he used to come home from work, eat, lie on the settee, watch the news, get ready and go out, and come home at about half-past-eleven on a night. I suppose he thought this was fine, but I was very unhappy. You just get pushed in a role, and you tend to plod along in it and you don't have the confidence to change it.

Betty's involvement in politics began in the seventies, after the move to the 'posh' new house. The area had few facilities on its doorstep. There was no bus service, shop, library or post office – there wasn't even a postbox. All this contributed to the sense of isolation, and in reality the community was set apart, as few people had cars in those days; although Betty did manage to scrimp and save to get an old banger, but that wasn't until the early eighties. But by this time Betty had come out of her shell. She had become the branch secretary at her workplace for the large Union of Shop, Distributive and Allied Workers (USDAW). She had learned not only how to fend for herself, but how to fight for others as well.

Queen Coal

Because we had nothing where we lived, I decided that we needed a mobile library and a post office and a bus service; this was in Windhill at the new house in between '74 and '84. A friend at work said that to campaign you really need to join the Labour Party. So I did, but they were all bloody academics apart from me at this small Labour Party branch. They said, 'why have you joined the Labour Party?' I told 'em that I wanted a post office and a library and this and that, and they decided that they would help me campaign. It took time but at the end of the day we did get a mobile library. We got a bus service to take the children down to school and back in the winter – before that they had to walk down the woods.

After a few years we did get a post office, but it were down the road. What we got near our house was a letterbox. I came home from work, and I was really excited because I knew they had been doing the letterbox that day. I came around the corner in me car and there was this letterbox, but it had been painted blue, and I thought, 'oh shit'. I went in and I said to the boys, 'I don't bloody believe this, all this time to get a letterbox and somebody has gone and painted it blue.' They said, 'Yes mum, we did it, we thought it looked better than red.' That was Donny and Michael. I suppose the lads meant well.

Betty sees the strike of 1984/5 as a defining time for her. It was those twelve months that finished the job that her early dabbling in politics had begun. She discovered a community of like-minded women. There was no turning back, no more lonely tears in a slum.

When '84 came along I had started to work part-time in the Feb. Mainly because the company had moved my job, and because I was the branch secretary of USDAW, I could only have this so-called 'new' job – which was my old job revamped – if I gave up being branch secretary. Well, I wouldn't give that up, so they put me in this office and the manager was really horrible.

We had an agreement that staff went on a training rate for three months. After the three months, if the work was satisfactory, then they got the rise to the full rate. If it wasn't, we looked at what the problems were and how we could address them. It was still a very anti-union company. We only got a union at Empire because of the legislation that every worker had the right to join a union.

I found out after three months that some girls that weren't reaching the grade were just being left on the training rate, and nothing was being done about it. So I had a meeting with the office controller and he wasn't at all happy, and we took it through the procedure and the girls were given the full rate. After that they were just gunning for me. I had had enough. So at the end of the day I gave up branch secretary and I was the union rep, but I said I couldn't cope and moved to part-time work. I was answering customer enquiries, and then I went onto telephones. If you like, we were the embryo of the call-centre thing.

Early on in the dispute Betty decided she would do what she could to help. She heard about WAPC and she wanted to be a part of it. She had already had local battles with some of the union officials, who insisted that the soup kitchen should provide food only for the miners and not their families. Betty was having none of that; she knew that the women, and particularly the children, would need help as well.

When we hit '84 I decided that I wasn't going to sit and cry any more. I decided I was going to do something. We had this little place called Windhill and Woolley Colliery Community Centre. I said I thought we ought to do meals for the striking families. I talked to a local NUM guy, who said they were only feeding the pickets in a soup kitchen and not the women and kids. I said that's wonderful, but what happens when you've got a single parent who's a striking miner? He says, 'Oh yeah, if he goes on picket line he can come but it's only for pickets.'

So then it was up to us to make sure the women and children got fed. What they were saying to me was, there's a soup kitchen in Barnsley and they can go there. Well, at that time it was 2p bus fare to Barnsley, and I said, 'So you get a three-year-old, give him 4p, and say get on the bus, cross two main roads, have your dinner and cross two main roads back?' I said 'No way: we are going to make sure that the women and kids are fed.' So they decided that we had to have a meeting at the miners' welfare. There was about three of these union guys who said you can't do a soup kitchen, you've nowhere to have it. I said, 'Yes we have.' 'Well, you've no cutlery or crockery.' I said, 'We have.' 'And you've no support.' I said the community will support itself, don't worry about that; even if we are only open for two weeks we will open. Well, social services won't give you permission. I said, 'Well they already have done.'

In the end they brought their bloody wives in to sort me out. Well, no way was that going to work: if the NUM men couldn't sort me out the bloody women couldn't. I don't know why they were against it. Not the whole of the NUM was like this, it was just a little group. I think they thought, 'We will control the strike we will say what is done what happens. We will do what needs to be done; we are not having any interference, particularly from women.' That's how I interpreted it.

Once again, Betty won the day and the centre provided food for miners and their families. She had heard of a mass demonstration of women in Barnsley, part of WAPC. It was the beginning of a new chapter in Betty's life. The relationships she forged in the ensuing months were to remain with her to this day.

We had opened the soup kitchen, and then we joined the brilliant women's demo in Barnsley. My friend and me made these placards, and off we went. Just doing the demo and the soup kitchen wasn't enough for me; I managed to make contact at the rally and found out that Women Against Pit Closures had organised this, and they were having meetings every Sunday afternoon in Barnsley. I went along to this first meeting, and the people who organised the meeting were obviously now getting in funding. And they said to me, 'What are you doing in your community?', and I said, 'we've opened a soup kitchen in our area' and they asked, 'Where are ya getting yer stuff from?', and I told them we were getting money from just knocking on doors and asking people if they could spare a bit of food.

They said, 'now you'll not have to do that any more. The group will support the soup kitchens, you come to the meetings every Sunday, and we will give you the money to buy the food'. Which was brill. They decided we had better arrange a picket, and I went home and I thought, 'he's going to go spare'. I said to him, 'I have been talking to the women at the meeting and they have decided they are going into Notts on Monday night and are going to do a picket.' I held my breath and said, 'I am going to go wi'em.' And he didn't say anything. I was amazed, utterly. He just looked at me as though I were a piece of furniture.

After that I was working in the afternoon – half past four while half past eight, I was coming home and sort of having me supper, then we would meet about twelve, go into Notts on the picket line, then come home and do the soup kitchen; and because we did a luncheon club for the elderly twice a week we could only do meals three times a week in the soup kitchen. We used to do that, and then we used to do shopping for the kitchen in between. I used to do the cooking with the women. Those from the community were brilliant. They used to come along and say, 'I'm not one for going to meetings and no way would I go on picket line, but I am more than happy to work in kitchen. You go to meetings and on picket lines and bring the money in, but we are quite happy just working in the soup kitchen.'

We ended up going all over the country speaking, and then going abroad. I hadn't done public speaking before, only at a small union meeting, never to such huge crowds as we did. And the first one we did was at the GLC in London. Ken Livingstone, who was then head of the GLC, had arranged it. Valerie Wise – the Labour MP Audrey Wise's daughter – had arranged it. It was the first time any of us had spoken, and I said to Jean McCrindle (treasurer of WAPC), who was with us, I said 'I have written this speech, what do you think? You'd better look at it'. And she said just get up and do it. I was horrified – I thought 'am I going to say something I shouldn't?'

We all did our bit, and then Valerie said 'are there any questions?' Well this guy got up, and he went on for about ten minutes, and we hadn't a bloody clue what he was talking about. We didn't understand the words he was using, we didn't know what he was saying, and we looked at Jean and the academics that were with us. They were all with their head in their hands . . . we thought, Oh gosh! Valerie immediately recognised this problem, and moved it on for the next question. He was just on his own soapbox, he wasn't asking a question. We sat there, and I said, 'What are we going to do?' Ann said, 'Don't let him get away with it, whatever you do.' So Valerie was starting to wind up the meeting, and keeping away from this guy, and I said, 'I would like to answer that man there', pointing at him. I stood up and said, 'We are miners' wives, love, we ain't had an education, we don't understand a word you've said, we don't know what you are talking about. But when this strike's over, we'll go and get some education, we'll come back, and we'll answer yer question.' I just sat down and I thought, 'I hope he doesn't say anything else'. I have no idea who he was. It was somebody that had come in to have their say. I think that gave us confidence. Everybody was clapping and cheering.

I thought of that when I was in Mumbai [formerly Bombay] with Anne [Scargill] recently. I had spoken, this guy stood up and asked a question and I could field the answer back at him. That was a wonderful feeling. That wouldn't have happened if it hadn't been for the strike.

For all her new-found toughness, Betty was still a woman's woman. She loved clothes, even if her budget didn't stretch to haute couture. Her work in a mail-order firm helped, because staff got a discount. She liked to dress well, and in the very early days of the strike, going out to see some action was quite an event. I think she was a bit like me and couldn't resist getting a bit dolled up for the occasion. That was before she realised that there was a high price to pay if you tried to combine being a political agitator with looking good; she learned the hard way that fashion and fighting did not go well together.

Because I worked in mail order, twice a year we had a sale for staff and you could get things really cheap. I'd got these red leather boots, and they were gorgeous; they were high heels of course, at that time.

It was my first picket line and there were Avon and Somerset police there. They were alright at first, but all of a sudden they started pushing and pushing us. We were, like, on a square piece of gravel, and they were pushing and we were pushing back. Then we decided we had had enough of this, and we were going to go back home now, and we were walking down the road to get back to the minibus, and they were walking along beside us. All of a sudden the chin-straps were going on. I had never been in that situation before, but I got a sixth sense and I said to the girls, 'There's going to be some trouble.' And all of a sudden they started arresting women. They arrested Lyn, who had got a little baby at home, and I said to them, 'Please don't take her, she's got a little baby – take me instead.' 'Well,' they said, 'she didn't bother about the bloody baby when she came here did she?' They arrested four, including Anne [Scargill], who had to throw us the keys for the minibus. The women had been doing nothing – we were just walking down the road. When I saw them put the helmets and chin-straps on, I knew something was going to happen. They just pounced.

We found which police station they'd gone to, and we went to shout outside and let them know we were there. Jean McCrindle couldn't reverse the minibus, so we all had to get out and push the damn thing, and I thought, 'Bloody hell! We're all supposed to be bright sparks here, and we end up like this!' Well, I got back in the minibus and looked down at me boots, and all the leather from the bottom was curled all the way up the heel. Me bloody thirty-bob boots ruined!

From that day Betty had a new distrust of the police. Of course, it wasn't simply because they had a hand in destroying her footwear – although that contributed to her growing dislike. As with many of those caught up in the skirmishes, she had never been on the wrong side of the law. She had no experience of what power the authorities could muster, so witnessing it for the first time came as quite a shock. Her view was: 'If they are going to fight dirty, then so am I.'

One morning at Woolley Edge, police were really really heavy; all sorts of things had gone on. They had smashed all the lads' car windscreens. We had got back to the picket caravan and were serving soup, and this guy came in and he was in his fifties. All of a sudden they just laid into him. He'd done nothing. I ran out screaming and shouting. You know when the Nazis used to wear their jackboots? These policemen had jackboots on like the motorcycle police do, and all I could think of was Nazi Germany, and I was screaming, 'Leave him alone! Leave him alone!' They told me to shut up or else I'd get some, and I'm saying, 'You try it – you do it and it will be the last thing you do!' And then we had to wait for the ambulance for this poor guy who hadn't done a thing. They took him to court in Wakefield, I forgot what they charged him with. We went as witnesses. We sat in the front. Nothing was happening and everyone was getting agitated – then charges were withdrawn. The police were late, as they got lost and couldn't find the police station. Useless. So that was the sort of thing we were up against.

Another time we were on picket line, and you know how the police do this [crossing her arms over her chest as if to link up] when they have to hold the line? And the inspector was screaming, 'Hold the line, hold the line!' I don't know what my son had done, but they had got him. And I am screaming, 'You're not bloody having him, he's mine!' This is Glyn, the youngest. And so I was sort of standing there thinking, what can I do? Well, you know they are quite big, these guys, especially with their helmets on, so I thought, 'right, I'll go back a few feet and take a running jump and jump up at 'em'. So there I am, and they were holding the line and I am thumping them on their noses and on their chins, shouting, 'He's mine, you're not having him!'

In the end the inspector just screamed, 'Let him bloody go!' So I got him back. If you'd have told me before the strike that I would have done that, I would have said 'Oh no, not me!' He was mine, you know. Not only was I fighting to defend communities and a way of life in the future, but at that time I was defending my own, and they weren't going to have him.

Despite often being in the thick of the trouble, Betty managed to get away unscathed for most of the strike, unlike her wardrobe. She felt that the police had put up with her outbursts and bolshiness up to the last few weeks of the dispute. At this stage there was a growing number of strike-breakers, and tensions were particularly high. Relations between the police and the mining community were at an all-time low.

They stuck me until February '85. We were having a mass picket at Woolley Edge, and Barnsley trades council were supporting us. I was at the front – nose-to-nose with the police, giving them all that. Ry [Raisse] Page, a photographer, was with us. It was first time I met her. I am giving it to the police, I just turned round, and then, 'Whack!', straight on me kneecap. He said, 'That serves you right, you silly old git.' You know when you get a knot and you could really vomit? And I said, 'Silly old git you are, I'll show you tomorrow!' And the guys were saying to me, 'Did he do that with a bloody truncheon?'

I said to Ry, 'I'm going to have to sit down.' I sat down and we sort of hobbled back to my house. A girl called Brenda, who was the one woman imprisoned in the strike, was up in Nottingham crown court that morning, and we had promised that we would be there to support her as she was conducting her own defence. So my knee was bleeding quite profusely, but I wouldn't go to hospital. I said, 'We can butterfly stitch it and go to Notts, and then go to hospital after court.'

This knee was killing. We sat in court until lunch-time. I could feel these dressings were really soaking, and I knew we had to go. Ry said she was going to stop at the first hospital we come to, and I said, 'No you're bloody not! We are in Notts, they'll all be scabs – they'll cut me bloody leg off!' I said, 'we're going back to Barnsley.' By the time we got there, I couldn't walk. We got into A&E. Ry was there with all this photography gear, and the sister was an amateur photographer, so she was, 'Ah all these wonderful people coming to my department!' Ry asked if she could take photographs. The doctor said I had lost quite a lot of blood. He told me, 'You have broken your kneecap and we will have to admit you to put pins in.' I said, 'I am sorry, I haven't time. I am too busy, just pot it up and I will be fine.' And poor old Ry had to knock on the door and ask me husband to carry me in. He never said a word – he just sat me on the settee and went off to the pub.

Ry took a picture of Betty not long afterwards. Wrapped in a long raincoat, she is on crutches. Woolley Edge colliery is in the background. It looks as though she is wearing cowboy boots. I'm fairly sure they weren't what the doctor recommended, but then Betty will do as she sees fit. The strike was the platform from which she launched her new self. As I spoke to her, it was possible to see she relished the role she had carved out. There was absolutely no way that Betty was prepared to go back to the housework.

The men changed. Before the strike, if I went to the pub they'd just sit talking amongst themselves, and it would be 'Wot you want to drink?' Then when the strike came along, it would be 'How ya bin cookie, what happened on picket line?' It was so different – there were the men talking to me like they'd never done before.

Betty helped write a book called *We Struggled to Laugh*, produced by the Barnsley Miners' Wives Action Group in

1987. In it, Betty made it clear that, for her at least, the fight went on long after the bulldozers had come in and flattened Cortonwood and other collieries.

> The strike may be over, but the fight and determination to go on will continue until all these wrongs are righted. . . . I do know that it [the strike] certainly enhanced my life, broadened my outlook with regard to politics, trade unions and education. I am humbled and proud to know that I was involved in this great piece of history. (*We Struggled to Laugh*, p. 12)

Betty goes on to say that she was misguided early on in the dispute, when she said that after the strike was over she could catch up on her housework and decorating. She says, 'I have a purpose in life, many aims and goals to achieve now which I never had before.' (*We Struggled to Laugh*, p. 12)

Arthur Scargill wrote the foreword to the book, and his ex-wife Anne contributed a number of personal recollections of the strike. Anne was and is a close friend of Betty's. One poem by Betty in the book sums up the depth of feeling she had.

Betty's life was going through a major shake-up. She could feel a growing faith in her own abilities; public speaking became second nature. For all the hardship, she clearly enjoyed being at the centre of the fray. In adversity she had discovered her true nature and, in her view, a true calling. When she spoke, people listened; her words were noted, even recorded – broadcast or in print. She was not prepared to go back to the obscurity of faceless poverty. She did not forget Brick Row and the life she had endured, but she learned how to use those experiences to put her role in context. When she gave lectures she would conjure up those days to illustrate the now-forgotten reality of life as a miner's wife.

After the strike I felt more confident. I wasn't as nervous as I used to be. I could stand up to people. I didn't go home and worry about it. I became a lot more vocal, too vocal I think, sometimes. The first time I spoke at a university, I really dreaded going through these doors. I thought, 'These are all bloody clever people, and who am I?' But as I sat there with these students talking and answering questions, I thought, 'I know a lot more than they do.'

We went to a function and Jean McCrindle introduced me to Bob Fryer, the Principal of Northern College. I said, 'Hello! When this strike's over I'm coming to your college.'

And, true to her word, Betty did go back to school. Northern College is an adult education centre at Wentworth Hall, Stainborough, only a few miles from her home. It offers courses to adults with no formal qualifications who want to return to learning. There is a high level of support for students, and that was just what Betty needed. But first she had to sort things out at home.

When I went to Northern they wanted me to do Trade Union studies because I had done a bit of voluntary work in the community and social services. I felt as though I was being pushed into that, so I said no, I had had enough. I wanted to do social and community. The first day we were there we were asked 'What do you want to do?' I said I wanted to get my certificate and then go back and work in the community. They said what about uni, and I said, 'No, I don't want to go, I am just not clever enough.' The first essay I did when I went to see the tutor, he said, 'This is a first-class A-level essay', and I was offended, and I thought, 'He thinks I'm still at school.' I was really, really offended. And then as time went on I realised that I was capable of things. This was 1987.

I did social and community studies. Then I suddenly realised everybody at college was supportive – not only the students, but the lecturers and the staff. I was non-residential at first, then I started staying one night a week and then two nights a week, and then I realised there's a different life out there that I could be part of. But . . . I'm not going to be part and parcel of that life.

I met Bill, who became a very good friend. At that time my daughter-in-law had just had twins; one was ill and was rushed into hospital. I finished up at college with a baby about 4 weeks old and a toddler. Which was no problem to college. Bill and me arranged a rota of students so that if someone one wasn't in a lecture they could have the kids while I was in a lecture. And I thought, this is a different kind of man.

If I put all the washing in the washer, when I'd go back it would have been dried and folded up and put on top of the drier, and Bill would have done it, and I thought, 'Yeah, I don't have to stick the life that I have been sticking at the moment.' Things came to a head, and I said to me husband, 'I'm leaving home, I'm not staying' – this was the beginning of '88, just before Easter time. It was a horrific time; it upset me because of all the bitterness. My ex took it badly – he clung to me and cried, and he said to me, 'You are a very hard person.' And I said to him, 'I've had to be.' And I said, 'No matter how much you cry now, you will never ever cry as many tears as you've caused me to cry', and I just went.

But then it was a case of us getting these phone calls all the time at college. He wouldn't get off the phone, and if I put the phone down he would ring again. It was a payphone in the annexe student accommodation, so if I left it off the hook it meant that other students couldn't get calls. I was still doing his washing and ironing, mind. Still going collecting the washing, taking it to college and taking it back, more for my son Michael than him. My ex rang up one day and he needed a new Hoover; he wanted me to take him in to Royston to get one. So I took him in and he got the Hoover, and when we were going back to car he said, 'I want you to come back,' and I said, 'Never ever.' So he said, 'There's only one person I can go to now, and that's your mum.'

Now, as I've said, my mum was the old-fashioned kind – you know, when you took your wedding vows, and whatever happened, you stayed in your marriage. And all the upset would make her physically ill. She had just nicely accepted I wasn't going back home, and I said to him, 'If you are going to upset my mum, the divorce papers will drop through your letterbox', and he promised he wouldn't. This was on the Saturday; on the Tuesday I got a call from my mum, absolutely heartbroken. He was there, in tears. She said, 'This lad's on his knees; he's begging you to go back,' and I said, 'That's it, Mum.' And I filed for divorce straightaway. She was in her eighties, and that was bloody cruel.

I had always had it in my mind that the children wouldn't always be little, but until my mum was no longer there I wouldn't leave home, because I knew what it would do to her physically as well as mentally. But in the end off I went.

Although Betty had talked a lot about Donny and Glyn, she had little to say about her son, Michael. I only saw one picture of him, in the living-room. When I asked about him Betty became unusually quiet. By the look on her face, it was clear that something terrible had happened to him.

Michael was dead. His life had been dogged with the epilepsy that was diagnosed when he was a child. The condition could generally be controlled if he took the correct drugs. Perhaps because of the illness, or a sense of hopelessness, Michael became a heavy drinker in his adulthood. He would get so drunk that he couldn't keep down the medication, or he forgot to take it. Michael had chosen to stay with his father when Betty left for college. She had offered to take him with her, but perhaps it was a relief that he didn't want to come, although I don't think Betty would admit as much. Trying to care for someone who does not care for themselves – especially a grown man who is much larger than you – is a tough job. Michael made his choice, and in truth Betty had reached the end of her tether with him. But that does not alleviate the guilt she feels. Nothing can be worse than having lost a child; for a parent they are always your 'little ones' no matter how old they are. It was the one subject that made Betty withdraw back into the dark cavern of her past.

Michael was my eldest boy. I lost him when he was 38, and he was a severe epileptic. I wasn't there because by that time I had left my husband. I had problems with Michael as he was drinking so much. He used to come home some nights and I used to be up an hour trying to get the tablets down Michael. I said to the GP, 'What am I to do to make sure he takes the right dose?' The GP would say that at the end of the day he has got to have his tablets, and he knows the result if he drinks, and there will be no blame attached to you.

You can only take so much. And by then I was at college. At first I wasn't residential, and then I decided I would go residential and asked Michael if he wanted to come with me, as men and women with children can go and study up there – the children are given accommodation. They have a nursery and if they are too old for nursery, they can go to the local school. Michael knew that his dad was a heavy drinker, and if he went there then, well, he knew they would both drink a lot. I used to go over and see Michael. He was in a difficult position, because his dad was so bitter against me because I dared to leave home.

I just couldn't handle him any more coming home drunk every night, refusing to take his medication, fitting, wet beds, vomiting. I mean, he had been epileptic since he was 5 years old, and I just couldn't help any more. He wouldn't work with me with it. He just wanted to go to the pub all the time. I know it sounds awful, and I still feel guilty about it, but at the end of the day I had a life as well.

Northern College was more than a place of education for Betty; it was a roof over her head, her new home. It gave her protection from the old life she wanted to leave behind. She decided to move in and live there full-time, as the college was a form of sanctuary. It offered a release for Betty from the world she felt trapped in, and it gave her the tools she needed to build a new future. But moving from one life to another took some guts.

My ex was ringing up the college and threatening me, saying he would go to my mother or commit suicide. Then one day I got a call from one of his friends, who said 'We've been to the end of the drive at the college; we know where you are now.' I said, 'Good for you – come along in to college. I'm telling you now that there's been a prowler around at the moment, and the first stranger that's found here will get a thorough beating from the students before we call the police.' So that immediately stopped. This mate said, 'You don't know what you're doing to him, he's in tears all the time.' I said, 'Tough. I am sitting in the pub like he did when I was in tears.'

When I rang my middle son, Donny – he was married, living in Selby – I said, 'I'm ringing to tell you now before anyone else tells you that I've left yer dad.' And he said, 'Mother, you should have done it years ago.' I said, 'Yes love, but years ago you were small and you could only have a council house if you were married.' And I said, 'When it came to the crunch the only thing I could do was to put you in care, get a job, find somewhere to live, and then fight for you back out of care, and no matter how rotten a life we had, I wasn't prepared to do that to you.'

99

At college we did a two-year residential course – you did a diploma essay, Northern College certificate, and diploma. And the diploma is the key to unlock the door to uni. At the beginning I wasn't going to uni. And then I sort of amazed myself, because I joined the process and I got offered a place at Edgehill, Bradford, Sheffield and Leeds Uni. I thought, 'This girl's got something up here.'

We were sitting talking at Northern one day, and a mate said, 'What you going to do?' She said, 'Oh, come to Sheffield wi me', and I said alright then. She said, 'What subjects are you going to do?' And I sort of just drifted along. Even in our year there were two ex miners who were doing really, really well, and you think, there's a lot in these coalfield areas that nobody gives credit for, and it takes something like that, the strike, before people realise their potential. I did Sociology and Social Policy.

Betty got a grant to go to university, and she worked at the weekends to help pay some of the costs. She got her degree, a 2.ii, despite having to deal with various domestic crises that got in the way of her studies. Her close friend Bill became seriously ill with failing kidneys, and needed nursing. On top of looking after him, she fought to get him the equipment and carers he needed so he could stay at home. He died in 2003.

Betty's graduation day was her proudest achievement. It was her way of waving two fingers at all her detractors, but more importantly of showing what a humble miner's wife could do.

I know my parents were dreadfully disappointed in me and my marriage. So when I went to uni, well, we had lost dad, so he wasn't there, but mum was there. Her face was just unbelievable, because they had sat mum right at the front, and there was all this pomp and ceremony, and as I walked back I went past mum and we were both in tears. She said, 'Your father would have been so proud of you if he was here.' I felt it was an achievement for me, for Women Against Pit Closures, and it was an achievement for mum. I think at that time I was the first one of the close family that had graduated. I had an uncle who was very clever, and when I look back now mum used to read and write very well. Lots of women were denied opportunities in those days.

These days Betty still works in a call centre to help make ends meet. She does a lot of public speaking at schools and colleges, as well as charity work. Betty is heavily involved with WAPC. In that group she has some of her closest friends, and an important outlet for her rebellious side. She is happy to tell her story; she wants people to know what life was like for a miner's wife, so they can see how it has changed and can learn from her experiences. She is also a bit of a celebrity in her home territory. I discovered this when she treated me to Sunday lunch at the local Salvation Army meeting hall at Hoyland Common, near Barnsley.

I had never been in a Sally Army place; it would not have occurred to me to go somewhere like that. Previously, I had dismissed these Christian soldiers as an annoying group of happy-clapping people in stiff uniforms, tapping tambourines and trying to squeeze donations out of passers-by in shopping centres across Britain. I was in for an education. The local Sally Army was based in a shed that resembled a scout hut. It looked as though it had been built since the Second World War as a temporary measure, a prefab. The intention would have been to put something more permanent on the site as quickly as possible. More than fifty years later the bulldozers and builders are yet to arrive.

From the outside it looked small, dark and unwelcoming; you would have quickened your pace as you walked past without giving it a second glance. So it was quite a shock when Betty pushed open the main door to reveal the tardis-like nature of the building. Inside, it gave the impression of being quite large, with a vaulted ceiling. It had to be big to cram in such a crowd. I was surprised to see the place was bursting with life and laughter. It was as if someone had thrown a switch and turned on a light so bright, you had to shield your eyes.

Large women and small men wearing huge aprons were sailing around fussing over tables that were overpopulated with an assortment of people. There were jolly pensioners waiting patiently, and hungry children with Sally Army band uniforms on whose mouths were opening and shutting like so many baby birds in a full nest. The air was heavy with the smell of meat and two veg. The similarity to school dinners didn't stop my tummy rumbling in tune with fifty others.

When Betty and I arrived we worked our way through the packed hall. Betty was greeted like a long-lost hero. There were choruses of 'hello' and lots of hugs for Betty, who introduced me as a 'writer' – the oohs and ahhs made me feel quite grand. Fortunately I didn't get the usual question, 'What are you writing about,' as no one was too interested. They had their minds set on getting everyone seated so lunch could begin. Small talk would have created an unacceptable delay.

It had the feel of a room full of starving people waiting for their traditional Christmas feast, who would do anything they could do to hurry its arrival. On that basis we were quickly ushered to the top table. Once we were seated, a solidly built woman in uniform called proceedings to order. She was clearly the boss. The microphone she used to get things underway was more like a symbol of power than a necessity, as you would have no problem hearing her powerful voice across the room. 'Welcome, welcome,' she boomed. 'Now before we start I just want to explain about our famous "all-in soup". We had a lady the other week who saw "all-in soup" written on the notice-board, so she went off searching for it from shop to shop, but couldn't track any down – now we all know why that was, don't we? Because it doesn't come in tins – the big clue being in its name.' There were chuckles and knowing blue-rinse nods. I presumed I was about to sample the delights of 'all-in soup'. 'I want you to enjoy your meal, and let us begin with grace. . .'

Thanks were given to the relevant authority for the food, and then it was a case of 'On your marks, get set, go!' As fast as the soup could be ladled out, it disappeared from the bowls. Lots of eager hands waved hopefully for seconds. The soup lived up to its name; it contained a mixture of all sorts of bits of meat and vegetables, inoffensive to the tastebuds and warming to the stomach.

The main course was Sunday lunch with all the trimmings. I didn't want my Yorkshire pudding, so the young band members sitting to my left pounced on it and divided it among themselves. It was the quickest meal I have ever attended. As I was still negotiating some meat and gravy, the plates were being collected by a slightly built young lad who had obviously pulled the short straw and was dishwasher for the day. The plates he was carrying were stacked so high in his arms that he tottered blindly across the hall, wriggling between the replete diners. At one point he almost had a collision with the boss lady. She steadied him and pointed him in the direction of the stacking table at the back of the hall that had buckets with ceiling-high suds for preparing the cutlery for the dishwasher.

As I sat among this mêlée, I tried to remember when I had last dined at a place where the simple things such as food and community took priority. And, in truth, I couldn't recall ever being among people like this. Old, young, able and disabled, all coming together to share a meal. Being a doubting Thomas, I looked for the catch, but failed to spot one.

The place had that wholesome feeling that our generation pretend to despise. It was like 'the Waltons meet the Last Supper'. And yet, if you could bottle up that good feeling and sprinkle it liberally around Islington's chattering masses, I have no doubt that hardened hearts would melt, a bit at least.

In this environment Betty was a star. It was clear that everyone loved and respected her. She even got extra helpings of potatoes to take home to reheat the next day for her lunch. My first reaction was to think this was odd, but on reflection I have never known real hunger, whereas Betty has. Most of us have too much food available to us, but when money is tight subsistence becomes an issue. If you have ever been hungry, you never take food for granted again.

The atmosphere in the place wrapped itself around me like a huge fluffy blanket, warm and safe. It was a timely illustration of what people in this area meant when they spoke of 'community'. I don't know how much lunch cost, but Cookie – who insisted on treating me – got plenty of change from a tenner. Not bad for a three-course lunch.

Betty went about introducing me to her chums. Her favourite was Lorraine, a lady in her forties who has Down's syndrome, but was nonetheless the life and soul of her particular table. She used sign language to speak to Betty across the room. When Lorraine came over she gave me a bear hug – it took my breath away. It was given without conscious thought; it came from the heart. I felt it summed up these people – in this glorified shed, what you saw was what you got. This was community in the real sense of the word. It felt like a huge safety net, as though you would never be totally alone, as you often are in big cities such as London. Was the price you paid a loss of privacy? Did everyone know everyone else's business? Did it really matter?

What it did do was make me rethink my view of the Salvation Army. Next time they interrupt my shopping I will take the time to put something in the collection tin.

CHAPTER FOUR

Life After the Coalfields:
Jackie and Don Keating

Of all the women I have taken with me on this twenty-year journey, Jackie Keating is the one who stands out as being the most different; her viewpoint is and always was poles apart from those of many of her neighbours.

What makes her a square peg in a round hole is her attitude to life. Her views are more in line with Buddhism than Bingo. Jackie has a hunger for knowledge and an innate belief that there is good in everyone, that we are all part of one global 'human family'. Oddly enough, the one person she had any doubts about was herself, although time and learning have helped prove to her that she was wrong. The woman I met in 1984 wouldn't recognise the contented, confident, opinionated person I sat chatting to in 2004. Today she is an author, a successful reflexology therapist, and an accomplished mum and grandmother with a solid marriage that has stood the test of time and many tribulations.

During the strike she was one of the few people I came across who refused to damn all journalists. As she puts it herself, 'To say all reporters were bad was just like saying all miners were thugs.' Her fair-mindedness proved to be an important contributory factor in providing the media with an insight that went beyond the clashes on the picket lines. Jackie gave an articulate voice to the real victims of the strike. I had the good fortune to meet her early on in the dispute, and it was thanks to her that I was able to portray the struggle from a perspective that took me into people's homes.

Her husband Don was a coalface worker at Cortonwood. He did not share her trusting nature, and was dead against journalists. He labelled us all 'wallies' and swore he would 'never have bloody press or telly reporters in his house'. I can afford to smile now as I type those words because, as it turned out, Don grew more open-minded with time, so much so that I think he is quite fond of me – he is certainly happy to sit and chat with me over a cup of tea and share some of the extremes of emotion that he went through over the years as a result of the strike. When the television documentaries went out on the twentieth anniversary of the dispute, the images they broadcast stirred up some painful memories. Don had to fight back the tears as he remembered what they had all been through. Like Jackie, he is an honest soul whose priority is his partner and kids. He is an old-fashioned breadwinner, the type of man you would want by your side in a tough spot.

The pair have been married since 1972, and when they began life together the future they looked forward to had nothing to do with collieries. They met while they were both in the Army. A barracks in Guildford is a far cry from working in a biscuit factory in Yorkshire, but fate and Jackie's 'hate–hate' relationship with her mother set in motion a chain of events that would form the bedrock of their lives.

Jackie has a difficult relationship with her mother Dorothy, or Dot. She found it hard to talk about their differences but, true to form, she felt it was better to be truthful than hide from the reality. Ever the pragmatist, she could see that it was her problematic upbringing that had helped to make her who she was today. She looks back on her childhood with sadness and anger, not aimed at her father – a hardworking miner to whom she did feel close – but at her mother.

Jackie, the only girl of four children, had it drummed into her that she was a clumsy fool with no promise or talent. And yet, as a young girl, Jackie loved books and would hide away in the local library reading as much as she could, away from her mother's critical eye and sharp tongue. Books released her from a world where she felt ill at ease, as though she had been parachuted into it by mistake.

I always felt like I was the cuckoo in the nest. I don't know why I was in that family; I've got three brothers but I am so totally different to them, and everything I see in them I want to do the opposite of. When I lived at home they would argue and shout, but I never did. I think sometimes that's a detriment to me, because I have never been able to handle an argument.

I was born in the front room of a terraced house, my elder brother was born there as well. This was in the early 1950s. We moved to a new council house and it was considered to be very posh as it had an indoor bathroom. No more having to use a tin bath! We'd got three bedrooms, two of them with a coal fire upstairs. There was also gaslighting and a gaslight right outside front door. Which my mother thought was totally amazing.

When I think about my mother, I realise that she was jealous of me. I don't know why she was like she was. I knew she didn't like her dad; she used to say to me how she hated him, but she never told me what he had done wrong.

I think my parents struggled for money quite a bit. I remember them going and finding pennies for Dad to have five cigarettes from slot machine kind of thing; but then again, Dad could never handle money because when he did have the money, he'd go and gamble it. That's what was rife round here.

It got worse; I was always reading books what were far above my age, and Mum would make me put them down: 'You're trying to be better than you are.' My dad was not allowed to hold my hand because of her. He'd come along from the mine and I'd go down the road and meet him, and we'd hold hands till we got to corner and it was by mutual consent we dropped hands and walked apart, 'cos if she saw us there'd be hell to pay.

I don't know why, I never understood it. After my youngest brother Alan was born – it must have been 1964 – she kept me off school to look after him. I remember her going out to work in a KP nut factory. Do you know, almost every day I got a good hiding because she'd had to go out to work 'cos she'd got kids, and that was the only reason. She would hit me around the head, but never when Dad was there. She was never allowed to hit me if he was around. If I told him what she had done she would always justify it. That were what it was like being brought up with me mum. Every time Dad wasn't in she was saying, 'You're stupid, you're a lummox, everything you touch you break', and it sort of fulfilled itself, 'cos every time I touched anything I broke everything. I was very, very clumsy.

One side of me feels all of this is awful to tell you, but it is the truth. At same time I should be grateful, because I wouldn't have been who I am without all of that.

It was funny, because I spoke to one reporter a number of times during the strike, and he saw me as a very well-educated person from a miners' village, and truth is I was not, I had the potential to be, but I came from a background where my education was not encouraged. That was due to my mum. I don't know where she got that from, as my memories of my grandparents are wonderful. I've got no horrible memories of my grandparents at all, but with regard to my mum that is totally different. Don says, 'You were brought up with total mental cruelty.' Not with love at all.

My dad died four years ago. He was a miner, a wonderful man. His name was Jack, Jack Hargreaves; he came from a place not far from here called Horson Street. It's all flat now, but everybody who lived in war at time always knew the

Horson Street Crowd. There was this terraced housing looking over the canal, and everyone knew everyone else and everybody was in everybody's house. It was a very tight-knit community – people would bake and share their food. If a child fell down and hurt itself, others would help them up. The other side of that is, it was a harsh community. If you got out of line, you'd get a hiding. Me dad always used to say his dad would give him a good clip if he deserved it and if you came home from school and done something wrong, you got another one. You got it from the schoolteacher and you got it at home as well, but he said it never did him any harm.

My dad worked very, very hard from being a young man. I think he was just 14 when he went down the pit. He was a very young miner, very hard-working. He did everything, he got involved in a blast just before the strike and the detonator went off too soon and blasted his ears. He lost a lot of hearing, but he still went down. At 37, when he'd got four children, his doctor told him he'd got such a bad chest he should come out of the pit, but he said 'I'm not. I shall bring my children up.' He was so steadfast and determined.

My mother believed I should go to a factory, or in a shop, or get married and have children and that'd be the end of it, but I knew I'd never, ever marry anyone from my area. Don't ask me why, but I just knew I would never marry a miner, which Don wasn't when I met him. I have only been out with two men – someone called Bill and he was from Sheffield and I met him on a bread van; and the other one was Don. I met him when I had joined the Army.

Jackie says her mother railroaded her into joining up. She was a very sheltered nineteen-year-old, she had never ventured far – shopping in Barnsley or a job in Woolworths was about the sum of it. She had not done as well as she could have at school, discouraged as she was by those at home.

Me mum wanted rid of all of us. Me brother was forced to go into the Coldstream Guards, I was down to join the Army; we were all brainwashed, basically. I hadn't got a clue what I was letting myself in for, I was so naive. Up to that point I'd only worked in Woolworths for a short time. I'd spent two years working in Halifax in a biscuit factory. I'd just got this wonderful job working with mentally handicapped children and adults in the special care unit, but I had to take a huge drop in money compared with the factory job. Mum was livid; she kept going on about 'I was in the land-army, it's the making of you.' It weren't until afterwards I found out that she was in the land-army, okay, but in the kitchens preparing veg. So I went down south in 1972 to join the Army. Me mum and dad put me on the train at Sheffield to Guildford. I had never been out of Yorkshire before that.

But it wasn't long before Jackie lost some of her innocence. Army life for a young female recruit was an education on a number of levels. Today she giggles about what she witnessed, but at the time she was terrified by this strange new world where casual sex was commonplace and female officers had their pick of the young women. Even today, as she spoke of what she saw, she did so in hushed tones, as though she didn't want anyone to overhear.

Luckily, or perhaps unluckily, I wasn't aware of lesbians up to that point. So seeing what went on in Guildford barracks was a profound shock, almost as bad as the other side of the coin, which was learning about women who were known as the 'village bikes'. You'd got these women who'd just go out with any fellas. There was this one woman called Randy Brandy. Anyway, one day she wouldn't get up, and you were all responsible for each other and you all got into trouble if the others didn't cooperate, so to get her out of bed we pulled these sheets off her, and I'm not kidding, even now I can see it in my mind all these years later: she'd got love bites where you couldn't even imagine 'em. It was awful when I realised that you were thought to come into one of these categories if you wore a uniform.

I remember when I was on night duty once. I was sitting at a desk and I could see into a window with lights on; there was a female sergeant undressing a female corporal. She had taken her bra off and was rubbing her, and I thought 'I can't believe this, get me out of here!' I was nineteen and had no experience of anything like that.

The first time we were allowed out after so many weeks training, I somehow got separated from the other girls and ended up with this Randy Brandy. She says 'Let's go in this pub.' I said, 'I've never been in a pub in me life.' I'd been out with my ex Bill a couple of times to a restaurant, or to the pub, but I'd never been in a pub on me own. We went in this pub and there was all these army blokes, millions of army blokes in there, oh and I'm sat there quiet in the corner. Don and several of his friends come and sat down near us. I'm all sort of dead embarrassed and thinking let me out of here. Then I caught me earring on something and it fell on the floor; Don got on his hands and knees looking for this earring and that is the beginning of me and Don. We started seeing each other, and he wrote this beautiful letter to me proposing. I'd only known him four weeks.

Don was a lance sergeant due for promotion; he was a career soldier. But his views changed when his work took him to Africa. When his unit flew back into RAF Brize Norton the wife of one of his team had brought their little boy to meet 'daddy' off the plane. But to everyone's embarrassment the child made a terrible fuss and would have nothing to do with him, probably because he had been away for a while. The man was devastated. Don was disturbed by what he had seen and decided that if he ever married he would never leave his wife and children like that.

So the army life was not for either of them. The pair moved to Yorkshire and for a few years were unsettled. Jackie says they moved twelve times in two years. Despite deciding not to start a family until Don had got out of the army and got a new job, Jackie quickly became pregnant. Not that they minded; Don was five years older than her and wanted children.

After the toing and froing they headed for Jackie's home territory in the Dearne Valley. They moved to the village of Brampton, in the heart of a mining community. Don got work as a miner at Cortonwood, and as a part-time fireman. For a while their lives chugged along at a steady pace. Don was bringing in a good wage. Their daughter Nikki was soon joined by a son, Darren. Life was good, and Jackie says they were a happy little family unit. That is, until the strike began in 1984. From that time events shook the peace they had created. It was to be many more years before some equilibrium returned to the Keating household.

The day Jackie heard Cortonwood colliery was to close and that there was to be a strike, something inside told her that life would never be the same again. How right she was; but nothing prepared her for how major the changes would be – some for the worse and some for the better. It is only with hindsight that it is possible to see the pros and cons of the events that were to follow the strike.

Like the other women she became involved in fund-raising, but she was always a bit of a maverick. Even a pie and pea supper for charity didn't quite go to plan. It was Jackie's idea and she only wanted to charge 25p per portion – so they would raise less money but ensure more of those in need could afford to come along and have some fun. But other members

The author in 1984.

The author (centre) with WAPC
at Riccall Colliery's last day,
2004.

Left: Bridget Bell from WAPC and 'PC Plod' at Riccall Colliery.

Opposite: Women's support groups demonstrate outside the NUM executive meeting in Sheffield on 12 April (from *The Miners' Strike 1984–85 in Pictures*: New Park Publications, 1985).

Below: A mass demonstration of women in Barnsley (from *The Miners' Strike 1984–85 in Pictures*: New Park Publications, 1985).

Above: Denise Fitzpatrick.

Right: Betty Cook in 1985 with broken knee, and with Woolley Edge Colliery, South Yorkshire, in the background (from *We Struggled to Laugh*, Barnsley Miners Wives Action Group, 1987).

Far right: Betty Cook in 2004.

Below: Local newspaper coverage of the women's role in the strike. Chris Fielding is central in the shot, sixth from left in front row, just to the right of Arthur Scargill.

Cover of *Counting the Cost* (Wharncliffe Publishing, 1991) by Jackie Keating, showing Jackie, Don and their two children.

Jackie Keating in 2004.

Hello, I'm the organiser of Hoyland Food Kitchen. Thank you for taking this time out to listen to our appeal. We are the Hoyland womens action group and we consist mainly of miners wives. These womens groups are totally independent, financially of the N.U.M. We're not complaining, the N.U.M have enough to worry about so the womens groups started fund-raising on their own behalf so as not to detract from the unions income & funds. The Government planned to starve our men back to work through their families by deducting £15 from the allowance for the wives and children. Everyone supposes we get £15 a week strike pay from the union, we dont, it is a Govt. imposed penalty on miners for striking. In my own case, my Sup. benefit is now £12.93 instead of £27, its a big difference when you go shopping, well, we dont go shopping anymore, we buy things as we really need them.

Everyone must now realise, this is no longer just the miners fight, it is the fight of the whole trade union. Thatcher & McGregor deliberately set out to butcher the steel industry and so reduce the support for the miners. She has planned for this strike for the last few years with Tebbitts law and by giving the Police all these special powers while no-one was taking notice and look how far its got her. She knows she cant win, for that one Iron lady, there are a dozen here that can match her.

There is no way she can beat these Iron ladies. We've had enough years of low incomes and bad working conditions to make us hard. Have no doubts, we are winning this dispute but in the meantime, we still need to eat. Our kitchen in Hoyland is open 5 days a week and we average 1800 meals per week to miners, their wives and their families. The kitchen is run purely on donations and we are desperate for cash. Our own local trade and communities as a whole, have been very generous. Although their trade is down because of the dispute, they are still willing to give and because we are also fighting for our communities, which become ghost towns after the closure of a pit, we decided to come out of our areas and appeal to those who are not involved in the strike. We are appealing, as a womens groups, for you to support us, every meal we serve, is another smack in the eye for Thatcher. Be it moral or financial, we need all the support we can get and we will continue to need it throughout the strike. We will win this fight for our jobs and we will win for the whole trade union. Please support us and enable us to keep the food flowing, it is starvation is the only weapon Thatcher has got, and we are not allowing her to use it.

United we Stand.

Speech given by Chris Fielding at the House of Commons.

National Women's rally, 12 May, organised by British Women Against Pit Closures. Chris Fielding is third from right, wearing a light-coloured jacket and holding the hands of two little boys.

Chris Fielding holding a WAPC T-shirt.

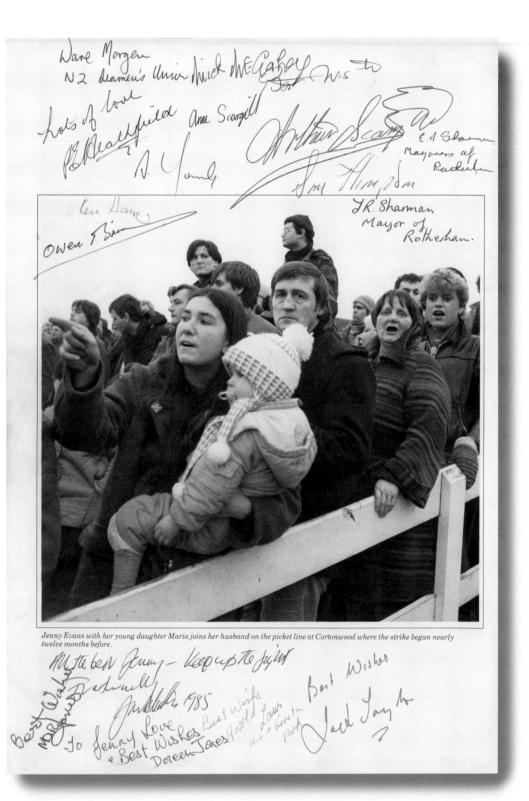

Jenny Evans with her young daughter Maria joins her husband on the picket line at Cortonwood where the strike began nearly twelve months before.

Harry and Jenny Evans with their daughter among the crowd at Cortonwood Colliery, and signatures of key figures in the strike, such as Arthur and Anne Scargill and Mick McGahey (from *The Miners' Strike 1984–85 in Pictures*: New Park Publications, 1985).

HOYLAND WOMEN AGAINST PIT CLOSURES.

XMAS PARTY

FOR CHILDREN OF ALL STRIKING,
N.C.B. EMPLOYEES WHO LIVE
IN THE FOLLOWING AREAS:-
BIRDWELL, HOYLAND COMMON, HOYLAND
ELSECAR, JUMP, BLACKER HILL &
PLATTS COMMON.

SATURDAY ⑮ DECEMBER
ELSECAR PARISH HALL.

0-10 yrs - 3-30 pm - 6-30 pm.
11-16 yrs - 7 pm - 10 pm.

Can you please register childs age,
name address and fathers workplace
to help with numbers for catering.
Phone 748504

Thank You,
C. Fielding.

ALL NAMES TO BE IN BY DEC 3rd.

Handwritten poster for a Christmas party.

Jenny and Harry Evans today.

of the women's action group wanted to charge twice that, to bring in more funds. There was a head-to-head, and in the end Jackie wasn't going to budge, so she held the event without the group. It made just over £70 and was hailed a great success. But Jackie was left with a feeling of regret that she had come to blows with the other women.

I found that story quite surprising, knowing Jackie as I do. She is such a gentle, considered soul that I can't imagine the sparks flying at a women's meeting. But then, at that time emotions were highly charged, and desperation changed how people behaved. There was tremendous pressure to do something to help, and people had different ideas about how that should be achieved.

I'm a reserved person really, and I found it so hard. You know, being this militant person, this person who was an enemy of the state. I mean, I've progressed since then – I can now be an enemy of nations, because being a white person I could be a great enemy! [Laughs] But joking apart, waving the banners and marching through the streets and all of that kind of thing was very, very hard. It's not easy to be a wife and a mum and love your family and just want the very best. I didn't want yachts and ships and all those kind of huge things what some people think you need. I wanted a home – a home, my family who was loved and cared for – and I am sure, I am so sure that nearly every human family on this planet only wants that.

It wasn't just Jackie who found it hard to assume the unwelcome and alien role of 'political activist'. Don, who had spent six years in the Grenadier Guards, was not given to lawbreaking. Quite the contrary – he had always been on the side of law and order, and had experienced first-hand what it was like to be under attack. During a tour of duty in Northern Ireland he had come face to face with rioters. On one occasion

113

Don came under fire. A crowd in Londonderry were throwing rocks and petrol bombs at troops. One of his colleagues and a close friend was hit in the face and had his eye gouged out. From that moment on, Don swore he would never succumb to mob violence.

Jackie says that is why she knew he was innocent when she received a call from him that she had been dreading – he told her that he had been arrested during running battles with the police. Having seen the damage it could do, she knew Don would not have thrown anything at the police – whether it be stones or petrol bombs. It was 18 June 1984 and Don was one of the flying pickets at Orgreave coking plant. It was a day that saw some of the worst violence of the year-long strike.

Don is a man who stands out from a crowd – literally, as he is 6ft 4. He had taken cover to one side of the main fighting, and other men had gathered around him. In a book about the strike written by Jackie, *Counting the Cost*, Don recounted the next moments in detail. He said that, as one of the men at the front of a group, he was pushed into the police line. As he fell to the ground a policeman – he thought he was an inspector – grabbed his hair. Enraged and in pain, Don shouted, 'I'll have you for that.' On cue, a group of officers grappled him back to the ground, punching and kicking him. His lip was split, and he was in such a tight headlock that he couldn't breathe and almost passed out. Along with many others, Don was taken to a bus and handcuffed to a rail before being taken to the police station in Sheffield. That day Don lost faith in the police. He says the violence he saw was reminiscent of the scenes in Northern Ireland; only this time the perpetrators were the police – supposedly the 'good' guys. Don was charged in the end with Unlawful Assembly, but he didn't appear in court until fourteen months later. The case against him was dropped – little comfort though, after having the threat of legal action hanging over you for so long.

Don's arrest affected the whole family. Jackie had also been brought up to respect the police; that vision of the friendly laughing policeman was shattered. Their children also learned to distrust and dislike the men in uniform. Jackie says both Nikki, who was eleven, and Darren, nine, cried. They didn't believe for a moment that their father had committed a crime, but they both feared he would be kept in prison or hurt in some way. These were feelings that left a scar. Jackie says when Nikki needed help from the police years later, when a man tried to lure her into a car as she went to school, at first she didn't tell anyone because she was frightened at the thought of the police becoming involved. Eventually, her distress was apparent and Jackie pressed hard enough to find out what was wrong and the police were called in. But Nikki retained her fear of the boys in blue.

Don's arrest was the worst moment in Jackie's life. But the fact that she stood by him – went to the court to show solidarity with him – actually worked in their favour. It helped to strengthen the bond between them. Out of the toughest of times came a deeper understanding of each other, and they were able to speak more honestly about their innermost emotions. It was a coming of age. Another life-changing moment for Jackie was when the police chased pickets down her road. She and Don had gone to help a neighbour, Jenny Evans, whose story is told in Chapter six. There were running battles between police and pickets at Cortonwood colliery, which was nearby. One of the injured men had made his way to Jenny's house. He had a deep wound down one leg, and it was bleeding profusely. He wasn't a local man, so Don had gone to find the miners who might know him and be able to get him home or to a hospital. He headed up the road right into the fray. There were bricks, bottles and rocks flying everywhere. Jackie headed home, but as she went down the road she heard heavy police boots pounding behind her. She says she saw one young man crumple to the floor after a group of policemen struck him on the head with batons and kicked him when he was down.

Fear took hold of Jackie; she ran towards the house. She was expecting to be beaten herself at any moment. Like the scene in a movie thriller, as she got to the door of her home and near to safety, her shaking hands made it difficult to get the key into the lock; then it wouldn't turn. As she fumbled desperately, Nikki watched at a window, ashen-faced and terrified for her mum. Once she got inside Jackie saw that gangs of miners were running from the police; neighbours were opening their doors to give the men shelter. She did the same. About seventeen pickets ran into her living-room, keeping away from the windows, lying on the floor or up against the walls.

There were these miners actually running into people's houses. They closed the doors and locked them, and they lay on the floor because we knew if those police came in, they would beat us up – and that includes women – they would beat us up. And I'm not kidding. It sounds terrible, doesn't it, twenty years on? But I promise you that was the truth. They would have, and they would have no compassion or compunction about it. And there's no doubt in my mind that they would have done it to children as well.

Now I've had to come to terms with that and sometimes, when I think about it, I do feel angry. But life's got a very strange way of balancing out – if you do real wrong you can hide anywhere, but you can't hide from yourself. You go home; that's with you. And I honestly believe when people drink or take drugs or all of this kind of thing, they're trying to hide from what they've said and what they've done. And in a way that's what I would need to let go, because I think, like a lot of other people, it's my way of coping. It's like carrying

116

around heavy bags and holding all of this in against these people was making me ill and making my life not worth living. But I didn't do any of that. I never hurt anybody physically, and I was always able to think, right, you're on your own – whoever you are, whatever you've done, you've got it. And even twenty years on, they may even think they can escape it, but they never will, because if they've physically hit somebody with their truncheon it's in their minds and they could never let it out.

I just could not comprehend what was happening. I was brought up to respect the police. All the time I was growing up, police officers actually lived in council houses among the community, so each time there was any kind of problem – a cat stuck up a tree or anything – a child would go to him. And as a father – because usually they were fathers with the same understanding – he was able to say, 'Oh right, come on, let's take you to your mum', or whatever. They was there as people, part of us. Now that has been superseded by those very, very aggressive men, and even now I don't have time for them.

Individually as people, if I meet them and they're actually okay, that's fine. But as a whole, police officers are nothing but aggressors in uniform, which gives them permission to do as they please. And perhaps somebody sometime will change that view, but twenty years on, that view stands. I saw their faces and they were enjoying it. A lot of them enjoyed it. Because, let's face it, policing, walking up and down streets, can be boring. It was a side of them what must be there, and this gave it expression. And perhaps it's a counterbalance to criminals, I don't know; but if you see ordinary wives and children as criminals there's not much hope for society.

Jackie says that for a long time afterwards she could not sleep and if she did, she had nightmares about the police. For her the world had become unsafe.

Don thought he had put the fierce emotions of the strike well behind him, but when the twentieth anniversary of the start of the action was marked in March 2004 with numerous TV and radio documentaries, he found all the old feelings that had been buried crept back. For him it was as if the events happened yesterday. The distress and fear were resurrected by the images of police and miners in collision:

> I thought I'd got over everything. You know, you move on, you retrain, you do this, you do that, and you start enjoying life again, and it's great. My life is great at the moment. But then there's these same feelings that were there twenty years ago. Where do they come from? You tell me. And I felt just as angry as I did then. I was sitting there watching the TV seeing a guy that went back to work and some of the police atrocities. I'm not saying that the miners were angels, because of course they weren't – we all know that – but all that bitterness came back to me, so it's still there. I mean, I've not thought about it for a long time. I'd sort of regressed twenty years in them few moments, and I really, really felt angry inside, bitter inside. Me stomach literally turned over, and I felt absolutely awful. These were feelings that I thought had totally gone. I genuinely thought I had let go and moved on. We've all got to do that, haven't we? But I felt dreadful, absolutely dreadful, and that is no exaggeration.
>
> I'm feeling it now because I'm talking about it, I think. I am sort of . . . Excuse me . . .

At this point Don had difficulty speaking, as he had to choke back the tears. The wave of emotion that passed over him was almost palpable. You could see him struggling to contain the anger that he thought he had successfully quelled long ago. He was disconcerted that he could not keep it in. I felt uncomfortable that I had been one of the triggers to bring back such painful memories to this gentle giant of a man.

I mean, I've never had a strategy for letting it settle down or putting it into the past. Like I said earlier, I'm really proud of what I did, and it's a great life experience. But something happens like that, time doesn't stop. You've still got your family, couple of lovely kids, so you get on with working, and you do what you need to do to bring money in to pay the mortgage, etc., to bring your kids up to a decent standard, and to start enjoying life again. And just by doing those actions, you know the past does tend to slide away. It doesn't disappear altogether. It gets buried in other things, doesn't it, you know? Then something comes along that gives you a real jolt.

You know it was just a shame . . . I felt it was a shame that so many people suffered – so many wives, so many miners suffered. A lot of people lost their jobs. A lot were made redundant. You see, going through that as I have done is terrible. I mean it's easy to say, 'Oh I've been made redundant,' it's quite a blasé thing to say, but having done it, believe you me, there's a lot to being made redundant. There's one hell of a lot surrounding that. You know, it's a massive step in someone's life if they're made redundant. And that happened to, at a conservative estimate, to 100,000 miners. It's an awful thing to have to face, you know. I felt sorry that it had happened. It could have been done a lot better. If people had to lose their jobs, it could have been done a lot better – I'm sure. All we were really asking for is a bit of decency, to be treated in a decent manner.

After the strike, Cortonwood colliery was closed and Don went to work at other pits in the area. It wasn't until 1993 that Don was finally made redundant, at the same time he was also made redundant from his job as a part-time fireman. It was a black day for him and Jackie; they were devastated. Don found himself out of work. He says he drove to a shopping centre and wept as he watched other fathers buying food and clothes for their children; he feared he would never be able to provide for his own again. It was an all-time low for the family. Don got a job stacking shelves in a supermarket. He felt degraded and demoralised.

I were walking round looking at people, and it was during that dark period of the three months after redundancy and I walked . . . I was seeing people buying things and I thought . . . I really thought it was the end of . . . I'm not saying the end in a suicidal way, because I can honestly say I never thought of that. Who's to say? If it weren't for Jackie, I might have got to that, but we'll never know that. But I really felt useless and unworthy. You know what I mean? This is about self-esteem, isn't it? And being kicked in the nuts and everything else that goes along with that.

I really felt that I was never going to be able to provide for my kids. A dreadful, dreadful feeling. I were frightened, absolutely frightened to death, just before I finished at the mines. I was generally a positive person, but I wasn't really positive at that time. I thought, 'Oh, what happens if I . . . I can't get a job?' You know, I'm knocking on a bit, as I thought – forty-seven-ish. What happens if I don't get a job? So my immediate reaction to that was use half of that redundancy to sort out the house. I owed £10,000 on me mortgage, so I went straight down to Bradford and Bingley and paid it off. I mean, that was the good thing about the redundancy, and that way I knew there'd always be a place for my wife and family.

I'm not going to get too involved in a discussion about Mrs Thatcher, because you know, well, we're living in the legacy of Thatcher now, aren't we? And I do get quite angry. I'm in the caring profession. I hope I'm a caring person; I don't like to use the word 'hate', but the truth is I hate . . . I still do, I hate the woman. I do hate the woman. And it's not because we lost the strike. Believe me when I say that. It's because of the deceit, the heartless way she went about things, you know. I mean, what a horrible woman – horrible, horrible woman. But I also know I shouldn't be saying that, and I should be above thinking about people like that. But you can't help how you feel, can you?

Don went on to retrain as a nursing assistant in the NHS. He works in a psychiatric unit and says he loves every minute of his job, even though he is being paid half of what he got at the pit. He says he wouldn't want to turn the clock back.

When the strike was over the men in the village decided to march back to work with their heads held high. Even in defeat they wanted to show they were not broken, but Don still cringes; he felt it would have been better just to go back without a fuss.

I felt let down when we marched back through the village. I really felt let down. A little embarrassed that we were going back. You know, we were going to win that and we didn't win it, and we were going back. I was proud that I stuck it out to that day, but there was no real glory in marching back through the village . . . Well, I didn't get there. I got down the lane and I was promptly turned back because, as you were aware, I was arrested on site, so I couldn't go in anyway. But no, I'd have preferred to walk back on a Monday morning for the 9 o'clock shift, or something like that, than march through the village.
With the closure of the pits, obviously people were fighting for their jobs and the jobs went, but what was actually really lost? Twenty years on, when you look back, did we lose something precious, or did we actually lose something which was pretty bloody awful?
Well, it comes down to the physical side of being a miner. My personal view is we didn't lose a lot, because nobody in 2004 should be on their hands and knees gobbling black coal dust, you know, with the fear of roof-falls and lumps of dirt

falling on his back. Nobody should live like that. It's 2004, for God's sake, isn't it, you know? So as regards that, then no. Maybe the community spirit of the guys working there – that was good; people did look after each other, because it was a job where you needed to. You know, if you were working there and Charlie Brown was stood behind you, he would physically watch your back, you know. So there's that loss that maybe the youngsters and the young workers today don't have, because they've not experienced anything like that within the community. I know I went on about, you know, the change of people within a community, which is good, but – I don't know – there was maybe a warmer spirit pre-strike, on up to the strike and up to just after the strike – you know, within the local club, the local community, the local shops. All that's changed. It's progress, but I don't necessarily think for the better. I don't think there's a lot in it actually, between one and the other.

Was it right to have the strike, to fight as you fought for those pits?

Knowing what I know now, and what I've gone through since the strike, I see that as really an unfair question. I genuinely see that as an unfair question. If I would be totally honest, then no. If I'd have known what I know now, then no I wouldn't have. . . it would have been a waste of time, you know. But I didn't know that then, did I? Same as I told you earlier. Redundant from the pit, redundant from the fire services as a part-time fireman, at virtually the same time. It was the most awful time of my life. I didn't know what the future held. And it's turned out okay. It's great, you know, it's lovely, but I didn't know that at the time. Up to now I work in the NHS, and instead of wielding a pick I wield a phlebotomist's needle; instead of driving a huge coal-cutting machine, I occasionally drive an ECG machine, which checks the heart-rates of patients. I work in a primary health care situation. We do health meeting groups, men's health groups, health awareness groups. You name it, we do it. And I love every minute of it, and until I wake up one morning and I think to myself, I've had enough of work, I'm going to carry on doing it.

So when you look back now, was the strike actually a good thing for you?

Let me just think about this a second. I sort of . . . Yeah, it was, yes it was. It was a good thing in the sense of the experience it's given me, you know. And I must have said two or three times, to the point of sounding boring, it was a great life experience, and I would honestly say it was a good thing for me. And you can pass on some of this experience to your children and to your grandchildren. But also being made redundant, although I didn't think so at the time, was a good thing for me; but of course that's with hindsight, isn't it?

When I finished at Maltby, there were a lot of lads there from Cortonwood, there were a lot of lads there from Silverwood, the Maltby guys, and there had been – for want of a better word – a booze-up in Elescar and we all went into town. There must have been a good eighty, ninety of us, and we were bouncing out of the five or six local pubs there, you know. And we all got smashed, and at one o'clock in the morning we were all sat outside – it was a summer's evening, in the middle of the road some of us – pissed out of our heads actually – and we were just reminiscing, and there were bloody grown blokes crying and all this, you know what I mean? That was great. That was absolutely magnificent, and these are the guys you're talking about. I miss that. But then you move on and you make new mates, and I couldn't fault the people I'm working with at the moment. They're a great bunch. That's what makes me enjoy I suppose, as much as I do, the job I do now. But you do move on, don't you, and you meet new mates? So, okay, you said what do you miss about it. Yeah, then I miss that but I don't miss the work; I don't miss the dusty conditions; I don't

miss sitting down and eating my snap-come-break in dirty conditions; I don't miss going to the toilet by scratching a hole in the muck at the side of the road, which is what we did. Some guys still do it, that work in the pits, okay. I have a collar and tie on now. I can have a cup of tea virtually when I want, you know. I can go to the toilet, I can wash me hands and then go to the canteen for me dinner. By God, that's good, innit?
And would you want your new grandson going down a pit?
   Absolutely not! [Laughs]

Jackie says that until the strike began she was asleep. She had withdrawn from parts of her life, plagued by the voice in her head that told her she was stupid – her mother's voice.

The biggest thing was me having to find out what life is like out there. I used to think that educated people had it all. They knew how to make good relationships because they had the education to make it work. It wasn't until I got out there that I realised their relationships were no better than ours. Whether they were reporters or professors, they didn't have a handle on life any more than I did. We are all on a journey, but you are fortunate if you have met a few people who have empowered you to think more and encouraged you to carry on.

Developing a broader outlook on the world would have been an alien concept to Jackie when she lived at home. Her mother, it seems, could not bear for her to do anything 'above her station'. One of the biggest disputes Jackie and Don had with Dot was about culture. Don has a love of classical music; his school had taken the pupils to operas and the theatre, and because of those experiences he developed a taste for the classics. On this particular occasion, Jackie says Dot was staying with them at their home. Classical music was playing on the stereo in the dining room:

My mother came into the dining room and took his record off. She said to him, 'Who the hell do you think you are? You are trying to be something you are not. And more importantly trying to make 'er into something she's not.' Don hit the roof. He said, 'Yes, I know what you think she is like, but you are wrong.' He couldn't believe that she had come into someone else's home and behaved in that way.

Needless to say, the couple tried to put some distance between them and Jackie's mother.

As Jackie says, the year-long strike gave her a big shake and forced her to enter the real world, where conflict and confrontation were realities. It also made her take a closer look at herself. There she was, a 30-year-old mother of two with a poor education and little confidence. But she had a hunger to learn more, to get something else out of life. She had left school at fifteen with no qualifications; she had a hit-and-miss grasp of the three Rs. She felt that after the strike she could not return to simply being a 'housewife'. But she was torn between her conditioning, which told her that education was wasted on women, and the impulse to fulfill something deep inside. So she turned back the clock and went to 'school'. Her saviour came in the form of the local library; she describes it as her 'favourite place in the world'. Here she tracked down an adult literacy centre in Barnsley. It took a lot of courage to go public on the fact that, at her age, she was not properly educated. But once she was in the centre the support she received quickly melted any fears, and transformed embarrassment into excitement. From feeling like a failure, Jackie began to look forward to a new future.

Her first 'essay' was about the strike. She struggled with grammar and spelling, but persevered. Jackie was staggered when her tutor suggested the work should be published; as far as she had been concerned it was just an exercise. Jackie had poured out her innermost feelings onto the page, and it hadn't occurred to her that other people would read it. At one stage she felt despair. 'I thought it had been a waste of time. Who wanted to read a book written by a housewife?' (*Counting the Cost*)

I believed that I was – it sounds very crude really – that I was thick and stupid, and that just being brought up in a mining community I wasn't very well educated. So I think I believed that if I went back to adult literacy course and got all the spelling right and punctuation right, you know, my life would become wonderful. I believed people who were very well educated had got a better handle on life than I had. Now, twenty years on and meeting lots and lots of people in between time, I realise no one's got a handle on life. While I was at the adult literacy course, I was sort of asked to go away and write something. And I said I hadn't written anything since I was fifteen – 'What do you want me to write?' And they said, 'Just write something about the miners' strike. You know something about that, but don't worry, no one's ever going to read it.' Huh! [Laughs] That just snowballed, and the more I said no, the more that just kept gathering momentum, which was quite funny really.

Jackie sent the manuscript to a few publishers and ended up doing some work for the Yorkshire Arts Circus, a charity organisation that showcases local stories. They struck a deal whereby Jackie worked for them interviewing people for different books; in return they would print twenty copies of her book.

The interviewing took Jackie into many people's lives. One of my favourite stories from her book is about a woman who was a homehelp. One day, while cleaning the home of a widow in her eighties, she found a Durex on the windowsill.

Curiosity getting the better of her caution, she held it up and asked, 'Do you know what this is?' The old lady said, dismissively, 'Of course I do – it's a condom.' Convinced that the woman didn't really know what it was, she asked, 'And do you know what it is used for?' The old woman was getting impatient by now: 'Yes I do, silly, it's for the condomsation.'

Counting the Cost did eventually find a wider audience when it was published by Wharncliffe Publishing in Barnsley in 1991. It was well received. It is now out of print, but I tracked down a copy in the British Library while researching this book. I never had the time to sit and read it cover to cover, so I had a bit of a surprise waiting for me when Jackie kindly gave me a copy as a gift when we met again in 2004. It transpired that she had written about me. I was the first reporter to interview her, and our encounters had made quite an impact. I was a bit worried about how she portrayed me; I felt I had been fair, but still it was strange finding myself being written about rather than the other way round.

I breathed a sigh of relief when I found she had treated me kindly in her book, especially as she wasn't too complimentary about other journalists. In my copy Jackie wrote, 'We met as young housewife and young journalist; twenty years on I hope we part as understanding members of the human family.' I think we do.

I wrote the book not because I'm an activist miner's wife. I was just being me. And to be quite honest, it was very difficult because my emotions were able to just pour out, and I was able to relive some of the experiences all over again. But then again it was very therapeutic. And I went on to discover that I could do lots of other things. I could be a youth leader. I did several other jobs, including working for social services, looking after other people; then I did something which I wanted to do from being in my teens. When I was fifteen I went into the library, and I'd read all the children's books in the library. I don't think there was anything I hadn't read at the time, so I'd gone into more adult, and I think I was fourteen or fifteen; I wasn't old enough to go into the seniors, so they said, 'Oh go and see if you can find anything in that section, you know, where you've got your geography and history books and that.' So I amused myself by going through several different things in there.

Then one day there was this book, and it was like a light came round it. I know that sounds really ridiculous. It's title was *Stories the Feet Can Tell*. I was drawn to it. The book was all about reflexology. I got it out, took it home and I read it and read it, and took it back and got it stamped, and reread it and reread it, took it back and got it stamped, and so on. I loved it. The librarian then said, 'Did you know there's another one called *Stories the Feet Have Told*?' Well, I kept reading that as well. I had that out and in and out. It was very old-fashioned in the text, and I just knew that's what I'd want to do. A few years ago Don got me my own copy of the books that are now bound into one.

Jackie's world opened up with those two books. If she had had more support, she might have chased the ambition to be a reflexologist when she was just fifteen. But there was no encouragement at home, just derision. Instead of pursuing her education, Jackie left school and got a job.

It wasn't to be. A miner's daughter was expected to go to work in shops and factories, and you didn't 'train'. And everybody else had got a different opinion of what I should do. Mum used to say to me from the earliest of my memories – although she hasn't said it recently 'cos it's never gonna happen – 'I've only ever had you to look after me in my old age, I never wanted you for anything else'. And after Dad died and I was up there one day cleaning, I put the hoover down and I thought, I'm fulfilling her destiny for me, I'm not doing it; and I walked out, and I didn't go back to doing everything. I only go up once a week, and I feel very, very bad about that, because a couple of days before Dad died, he turned round and he looked at me like that, and says, 'Look after your mum for me, won't you?' and I said to me Dad, 'You clear off', and I'm not, I can't.

For Jackie the experience of talking to reporters, doing TV and radio interviews, had forced her to see that she was not in the least bit thick. A part of her must have recognised that in fact she was articulate and quick-witted. The emotions of the strike were translated into a drive to achieve something for herself. She was a good wife and mother; she had been a loyal part of the community; she had done her bit for others. Now it was time to do something for herself. The reflexology books were never far from her thoughts. As the years passed, the idea of practising reflexology lost none of its fascination.

When I was forty I actually trained and passed all my exams. It took me all that time to get there, but I did, and I've had the most wonderful, wonderful life since. I wanted to be there for the children; I wanted to be able to have lots of fun with them, laughter and joy and baking, and we did. Nikki says to Darren when she was pregnant, 'I don't remember a bad day; I don't even remember a bad day in the strike, 'cos my mum and dad were always there for us, always,' and we did, we had a fantastic family life. It all changed with the strike, and it was probably my fault in some ways. If you've read the book, you'll know – I really wanted to do something else with my life. Although I still wanted to be a wife and mum, I didn't ever want to leave Don, I didn't want to leave the kids, I wanted it all – that was one of the things that came out of it.

Then one day Nikki came home and she said, 'Mum, there's somebody training in reflexology at Birdwell.' This was after the strike – it was a long time after the strike, because he'd got his redundancy, so we'd got through the real harshness of getting over the strike, and he says, 'If that's what you want to do, love, you go', and I paid £50 to this woman who sat there and poked me feet like this. I goes, 'What you doing?' having read it, and even from then every time I came across an article knew what I was talking about. She goes, 'I've got a teaching qualification, I can teach anything.' I remember saying to her, 'It's a good job you're not a brain surgeon,' 'cos she didn't have a clue. I came home and I'd lost all that money, which is a lot of money for us. Don says to me, 'If you really, really, really want to do it I will back you, I will – but do it properly.' I said, 'I will do it properly,' and I went back to my favourite place in the world – the local library, where I got all the information about the British School of Reflexology.

I became interested in all sorts of alternative therapies, alternative ways of thinking, because we're more than we think, we are. Don gave me £1,000 out of his redundancy. 'Flipping Norah!' he says, 'a thousand pound for playing with feet, I can't believe I'm doing this!' And he said, 'Do you really want to do this?' I goes, 'I really want to do it,' and I went to train in Nottingham for weekends, and then doing postal research I trained in Swallow Hotel for weekends. Now they've opened a place in Harrogate, it's for northern area where they've got a proper school, but in them days – that was ten years ago – they trained you in the hotel. You stay there. Some of the time I went to stay with Don's family, because they're from Nottingham. But the very first day I did reflexology the tutor said to me, 'Where have you trained before?' I said 'I haven't,' and from the moment I did feet it was like I've always known how to do it. Anatomy and physiology was hard because, leaving school at fifteen if you're training to be a nurse, you're around a lot of people who use the pronunciation properly and the terminology properly, which I was learning from a book. Although I understood it, I didn't always understand how they said things, which was quite hard.

Like the Tri-meagle nerve. I didn't know to say that properly. There's loads of medical terms I don't say properly, but it doesn't mean to say I don't understand it, 'cos I do, and Don said to me, 'What is it about you with your tenacity about this?' I says, 'I'm going to do it,' and it was hard. I really found anatomy and physiology hard, and I'd started working by this point. Part-way through the book you'd know where I'm up to, I'd been in the youth service, and we didn't earn enough money. I did two years in a lampshade factory, and then I went to Social Services, which was the most rewarding I think – but very troublesome in other ways. That taught me a lot about people.

Learning how people like management will pinch your ideas and pass them off as theirs, and how other people work, and the interplay of people is fascinating. The thing is, during the time I was training I believed that there was a force outside myself that would help me. I was finding it such a struggle, I couldn't tell you; and I remember sitting in the house saying, 'Please, please, if you're there I need some help 'cos I can't do this on my own.' I could do the practical, that's not a problem 'cos they said I was almost perfect from starting. Learning the anatomy and physiology part of reflexology, the professional course, made me realise that I wasn't thick and stupid; I could understand all of that. Practising of reflexology was wonderful. It's like I've always known how to do it.

Halfway through the course you are asked to find somebody to train on. Some schools you did dozens, but they believe that you should have a particular person, so I went to my GP and the reason I said the tri-neagle nerve is because it's when your eye drops, and it's not very favourable with modern medication really, and it does take a long time to go back. So I went to my GP and I said to her, 'Do you think you've got anybody who's got this kind of problem. Could you ask them? I'll treat them for nothing for several months if I can keep up with that.' She says, 'I can't see a problem, Jackie, come back in a week.'

So I went back, I said 'Have you got somebody?' She says, 'Well, not who you asked for, but I have got somebody.' I says, 'Well, who then?' She says, 'Me.' I thought, 'Bleeding her, this doctor, you couldn't get anyone tougher if you tried.' Then, halfway through treating her, she had a terrible fall and ended up in hospital. Well, I had to follow her and do reflexology in the hospital and at home. I still see her ten years on; she's my patient. I'm not hers any more, 'cos she's retired.

What happened was she had this nasty fall with arthritis, and she says to me – she was crying, and this hard doctor you wouldn't have thought could cry – she says, 'Jackie, my life's over.' And I said, 'Why are you saying that?' She said, 'Cos even my colleagues, my senior colleagues, can't do anything for me.' And I said to her, 'I will never give up on you; I may not be able to cure you, but you will have a life.' She says, 'What is the point if I can't do what I love?' I said to her, 'The one thing I've understood in the last few years is, it's not what our logical mind thinks, sometimes you're meant to do other things, and you wouldn't do it if you'd got the choice, you wouldn't do it. But perhaps you're meant to fulfil something else.' I said, 'I don't know what, you don't know what,' I says, 'but we've just got to get you out of bed to find out what.'

She says, 'It's pointless.' I says, 'You're not pointless to me; you helped me when I needed help, and I'm gonna help you.' I said, 'I'm gonna get you out that bed, and I promise you in a year's time I'm gonna ask you if your life is worth living.' And she said, 'It won't be.' I said, 'Yes it will. I'm not going to argue with you, you're just going to get better.' And I've treated her every week, apart from when she's away or I'm away and even when I'm away she texts me. She text me this week – I've been away this week – she text me, 'Missing you,' and I said to her, 'What do you think a year on then?' She goes, 'Not the life

I planned.' I says 'No', but she has helped so many people who have been battered and bruised at home and needed somewhere to go. She's organised the funding, the secret places for them, and I said to her, 'Is it worthwhile?' She says, 'Very worthwhile.'

A few months after I left work, I sat here and thought I was getting chicken. What was I doing just clearing off and just doing reflexology from home and just enjoying myself? I'm chickening out on life, and shouldn't I be doing more? I sort of asked, 'How come, then, if I'm just sat at home or sometimes I'm very, very happy, I'm very happy doing reflexology, then how am I contributing to the whole if all I'm doing is being at home?' And then I thought that if I hadn't been in the place I was to help this particular lady who helped so many other people, she couldn't have done that if I hadn't helped to get her better. I realised that I was a very tiny cog in a big wheel, in something what operates better without us interfering.

Had the strike not happened, I wouldn't be who I am today, and I'm a very different person to I was then. I feel now that I was asleep. I was willing to walk along with everybody else, all living this life. But now I don't ever read newspapers, and whenever I watch television of any kind of news, I always question it because, again, everybody's a product of their own beliefs or how they're brought up, so they actually come here with a preset idea of what a miner or miner's wife is. And I've tried to change that round.

Now, even then – I think looking back in them days – I think I always thought you had to be fair. You had to be fair and accept the next reporter that was coming along wasn't going to be like the last. And, yes, I did get burned, yes I did. But at the same time I was able to see my world from outsider's point of view, and sometimes all these people couldn't see our determination and our humour because, believe you me, miners' humour is very, very strange; but it's something what keeps us all going. And in times like wars, it's a dogmatic sense of self; it's what's needed. Well, it has been in the past.

It really was a war. It sounds so terrible, doesn't it, that one set of people was at war with another? But that changed me, because I realised that certain people in power could do that. They've done it twenty years ago and no one in this country, or anywhere else, are going to avoid being manipulated if these so-called people decide. If they want to change something, they're going to, and sometimes you're powerless, and we were powerless in that. A lot of people behind a lot of doors have sat there for a long time planning all that, and as an ordinary person getting on with your life, how do you combat that? They did – they had war references and nothing will ever make me believe any different. Maybe when some of the secret government files come out in future years this will be shown. But in the meantime, as people's minds been damaged by what they perceive to be terrible, terrible mining people, but just think, in twenty years there have been no problems in the north, so where have all these 'enemy within' gone? Of course, they never existed. They did me a favour, they woke me up; but not only to my life changing, but to what happens when powerful people are around. Hopefully there will never be any more wars. But I am so pleased to have been part of it. I never regret that year. I don't regret meeting new people, seeing life differently. It's moved me on.

Don has changed such a lot, and he's done lots and lots and lots of different things, and now I smile to myself because – in the book I actually said that – I'm attached to a man who was one minute a miner, the next minute a fireman, now I'm attached to a care assistant. I never know where I am from one minute to the next. But it's all down to titles, isn't it. And I've learned to give titles away. I don't think of people as coming from different religions or groups. People are just people to me.

Jackie qualified as a reflexologist and sees clients at her home. With her it is more than a job; it is her way of putting something back. She charges much less than the usual rate, in particular to the elderly or unemployed. And if someone needs to lie down and chat for two hours, Jackie is happy for that to happen. The pleasure she gets from her work is great. I would put 'chatting' quite high in Jackie's list of loves. Don says her clients are more like friends, and he is amazed at the noise that comes from her reflexology room upstairs – a bedroom freed up after the kids moved out. He says there are shrieks of laughter, and sometimes deep serious murmurings as they set the world to rights. Not exactly the totally relaxing, sleepy sessions he expected.

These days, the world Jackie and Don inhabit bears little resemblance to how they lived when I met them. Then they were what I would describe as a typical working-class family, with the emphasis on 'work'. They had money coming in, but they had to graft for it. And it's not that they don't graft now, but the whole feel of their lives is more middle-class. By that I mean their expectations of life have changed. Their home now resembles something out of a *Good Homes* magazine. The fireplace in the living-room, for instance, which had a copper hood in the eighties, now has an ornate surround like an Adam fireplace. The decor was pristine, and done in soothing pastel colours. Perhaps the most change was in their garden, though. These days Jackie has fairies at the bottom of her garden, quite literally. The plot at the back of her house is much larger than most of those on the row. She and Don landscaped it so there were different 'rooms', and in each one it was not difficult to spot little pairs of gossamer wings and painted eyes watching you.

Don had wanted to treat Jackie once the mortgage was paid off, so he offered to buy her the conservatory that she had been nagging him about for years. He was staggered when she said she didn't want one. He wandered off, muttering darkly about how he would never understand a woman's mind. Jackie laughs at Don's bewilderment. It was true that she had dreamed of having a 'garden room' like everyone else; it was all the rage in the eighties and nineties. But as the years passed she watched as those she had envied with their glass rooms got more and more hot under the collar. They struggled to deal with the intense heat, flooring never seemed to work, blinds cost an arm and a leg, and keeping the glass clean was virtually impossible. No, she thought, that isn't for me. Instead she opted for a platform in the garden, where she could do her yoga. It went with the koi carp pool, the delicate oriental bamboos, tree chimes and the gazebo. It was all a far cry from the 'hand-to-mouth' days, when the couple feared they might not have enough to feed their two children, never mind cater for exotic fish.

The image I carry of Jackie's house when we first met was of a the kind of place that is so homely, it makes you feel warm in the pit of your stomach. I particularly remember the fire in the living-room, coals glowing red and welcoming, hypnotic after braving hours in the freezing cold on picket lines in the bitter winter of 1984. Jackie recalls how one reporter had popped in to see her after having had a day from hell chasing the police, who were in turn chasing the miners. Ever the hospitable lady, Jackie went to the kitchen to make some tea. When she returned to the room the reporter had taken off his shoes, had his feet up by the fire, and was fast asleep. When he came round he was most apologetic, but Jackie was delighted – to her it was a compliment that someone could feel so relaxed in her home.

Jackie and Don work as a team. The years of hardship have been turned to their benefit. They learned valuable lessons and managed to put most of the pain behind them. An irresistible thought occurs to me: they are a bit like the Tin Man and the

Scarecrow in *The Wizard of Oz*. Don would be the Tin Man who found a heart – a softer side to the tough soldier alpha male, and Jackie found a brain, which – like the Scarecrow – she had always had but just couldn't see it, because she had been conditioned to think she didn't have one. I wonder if that makes me Dorothy, trying to find my way home?

The renewed confidence and understanding of life that Jackie discovered after the strike were to prove vitally important to Don. He felt he could turn to her for the emotional support that he had always denied he needed.

Before I was made redundant in 1993 I was a private person; I would never talk much about my emotions. I would rather put on my walking gear and go out. The three months that followed me losing my job as a miner and as a fireman were absolute hell. Again, I don't want to keep harping on about the redundancy, but you know, it was a pit redundancy. And of course the fire service, because I thoroughly enjoyed being a part-time fireman. I did fifteen years. It all came at once, and it was the lowest point of my life. And that's when Jackie taught me to talk. She made me realise the importance. She persuaded me to talk, and that allowed me to cope with it the way I have. And I think . . . I genuinely believe that I've coped with it okay. I dread to think what would have happened if it hadn't been for Jackie. I genuinely mean this – if she had not been the person she was at the time, and coaxed it all, and made me talk about things, I don't know what would have happened. And that's led to other things – you know, talking about other subjects which to me was taboo, which to me were part of my inner self I would never talk about before.

I lost a brother in 1981 – he killed himself, he hung himself. I've never, ever talked about that, and it was only after the 1993 redundancy thing, by Jackie making me realise that talking about our current situation, which was nothing to do with Paul, was a good thing. It was the knock-on effect of that – realising the importance of talking and getting it off your chest, and trying to cope with it. It made me see that I could talk about other things as well. Serious things really. Well, that certainly was. And I handle that quite well now, and I can sit and talk to anyone about that incident without being too emotional about it.

They do say that the best kind of therapy is to talk to your loved ones, if you're lucky enough to have them.

Absolutely. There's absolutely no doubt about that. I'm convinced of that, and I'd recommend it to anyone, I really would. It's worth a try, isn't it? It worked for me. I'm not saying it would work for anyone else, but for God's sake try it!

Jackie and Don are two people who have always tried to do the right thing. Their good fortune in finding each other so young is without doubt the cornerstone of their success; it is how they have survived all the bad times that life has thrown at them. They put their family unit first at all times. Today they reap the benefits of that priority. Theirs is a love that has thrived on the pollution of politics; they were innocent victims, but in the end they emerge as the victors, with a stable, 'paid-for' home, happy children, work they both enjoy, and the prospect of a comfortable old age.

I wouldn't want to be that person who was asleep. I was very happy, don't get me wrong. I was very happy being a wife and mum, I really was. But I'm still a wife and mum – incidentally also a grandma – but I'm able to be myself as well. When other people talk to me I respect them, and hopefully they respect me in turn for who I am. I'm not a miner's wife, I'm me.

138

CHAPTER FIVE

Making it in a Man's World:
Chris Fielding

A few years ago, when I was first putting together my proposal to write this book, I had to make the difficult choice of who to include. After all, there were thousands of women who fitted my particular bill. My criterion was that they had to have been on the 'front line' of the strike; they had to have taken an active part in the events of that year, both in the home and on the streets. They would be women I had known or known of, but not the 'celebrity' women who found fame or political kudos through the action. I did not want those who were parachuted into the coalfields and, once the action was over, headed back to their middle-class London homes to write their PhDs. They had to be women whose lives were directly affected by the loss of the pits – changed forever, for better or worse. To top it all, they had to have a strength of character that epitomised the spirit of the people I was trying to capture. They had to encapsulate the untold story of the women in the coalfields. I already knew a number of these women who were like the flipside of the men portrayed in films such as *Brassed Off*, *The Full Monty* and *Billy Elliot*; they were not silver-screen portrayals of imaginary people, they were the real thing.

When I looked through the now-faded photographs of the demonstrations in 1984/5 I spotted a number of familiar faces. One in particular caught my eye. She was a pixie of a girl, marching at the front of the crowd, arms linked with other women. She had short, jet-black hair, and was wearing a tight-fitting WAPC T-shirt on her small but solidly built frame. Her cheeky grin brought a smile to my face. I had a distant memory of her during the strike. I knew that she had been one of the young women thrust into the limelight, who found herself dramatically plonked centre stage.

I couldn't remember her name – only that she was from the Dearne Valley, somewhere near Barnsley, probably Hoyland or Wombwell. It took a few phone calls to some of the women I already knew. In spite of the passage of time, a lot of those who were part of WAPC kept in touch with each other, or just kept tabs. With the jungle drums beating, it didn't take long to come up with a name and general location. The young lass in the photo was Chris Fielding.

Remarkably, someone had remembered her and found her phone number in an old address book; whether it was still the right one or not remained to be seen. In the intervening years many people had moved on, so the chances were high that she may have gone. I didn't use the number straightaway – I kept it on a scrap of paper by the phone for a few days. I wanted to think things through before I put the call in to her. I wondered whether she would remember me, or even want to talk to me – so many of the mining families didn't distinguish between those journalists who treated them fairly and those who did not. Admittedly, I couldn't really blame them – I was often puzzled to see the yawning reality gap between what I had witnessed for the BBC and what was published in the newspapers the next day. I don't regard myself as one of those who dismissed the mining communities as the 'enemy within', but how were they to know that? Fortunately, my own background and the work I produced gave me the credentials necessary to open doors that would otherwise have been firmly closed to a reporter. Nevertheless, it was hard to phone someone out of the blue, no warning, and try to convince them that I was a good guy and that they should therefore share their lifestory with me.

I waited for a week or so before I tapped the number into my phone. I've no idea why I thought the wait would make a blind bit of difference, but somehow in my head it felt like a decent interval. What it did do was give me time to collect some information on Chris, to remind myself of who she was and what part she had played in the strike. I knew she had been very active, but I had forgotten just how much she had done. Chris was chosen to address a meeting at the House of Commons. For one so young she had given a remarkably eloquent and impassioned speech. I guessed that she would never have dreamed of doing such a thing prior to the strike. She had also been involved in one of the biggest soup kitchens, based in a nightclub, that dished up 400 meals a day for miners and their families. This was no wilting wife who stayed at home to peel the spuds.

I feared the passions of the year-long strike would still run high, that she might feel great bitterness; certainly other men and women I had met did. For a large number the anger was still as fresh as blood spurting from a severed artery. It was mostly aimed at Thatcher or Sir Ian MacGregor, but there was plenty left for the police and the media. My concerns evaporated when I heard Chris' deep, gravelly smoker's voice on the other end of the line. It had the ring of a Yorkshire Marge Simpson about it. Almost immediately, she was talking to me like a long-lost friend. She said she remembered me, and that helped as it gave me an immediate history with her.

She told me most colliers had moved from her street and the surrounding area: it was a mining town without the mines or the miners. Women had been left to sort out themselves and their children. Some men had gone off with other women, some had moved away to spend their redundancy money on starting up businesses, like bed and breakfasts in Blackpool. Some had died, some had just moved away to find work elsewhere. Chris's marriage had broken up as the strike ended

– although she didn't tell me the full truth about what happened until we met up more recently. She had spent the ensuing years doing her best to make ends meet and feed her two children. She didn't feel bad about it, though; there was no way she would choose to go back to her old life.

When her marriage ended she did fear that she was facing tough years ahead, on her own with two young children and no work, and therefore no money. She laughed as she remembered she had been worried that men would not be interested in a divorced mum. Chris was to find that quite the contrary was true. A chuckle crackled down the phone when she told me she had men queuing up to take her out, and all of them years younger than her. 'You know what, lass, right now as I'm talking to you I've got a toyboy upstairs putting shelves up in bedroom. I'd rather have that than what I had before strike.' She was more than happy to speak to me. She was one of those people who just couldn't see what all the fuss was about: live and let live. I had intended to drive up from London to see her in the following months but, what with one thing and another, it was to be four years before I actually made it to her house. Luckily for me, Chris wasn't a stickler for punctuality.

When I eventually got this project going she was the first person I went to interview. I could see many parallels between Chris and myself beyond our closeness in age. Like me, she had been a single mother for years; she had also entered a male workplace and proved she could outdo the men on their own ground. As you will read, she succeeded on all fronts. I wondered if she had changed much. Certainly, she sounded as cheery as ever, although her voice had dropped a pitch or two – it had that deep, sexy tone of a lifelong smoker. She had moved since the end of the strike, but not far, only a few streets away. Twenty years ago she was a fresh young face in the crowd of angry women. She was always enthusiastic; the pictures of her at rallies at the time are enlivened by her presence.

After a lifetime of taking on all comers and giving them a bloody nose, it turned out she was in the midst of another fight – the mother of all battles, as it was coming from within. She was in the secondary stages of multiple sclerosis (MS), a disease that attacks the central nervous system. It was typical of her, though, to treat this scary condition as an 'embuggerance' more than anything else. MS, which predominantly affects people aged between twenty and forty, can cause severe disability, although it varies from patient to patient. Chris dismissed it as a bit of an annoyance.

Chris was only twenty-six when the strike began – a few years older than me – but she had already had a bellyful of life. Her story humbled me.

Isn't it odd how wrong we can be about the world we encounter? We put on our own brand of spectacles and see things as we want them to be, rather than how they really are. Well I do, anyway. During the strike I happily built the picture of Chris and her contemporaries as committed, loving and loved miners' wives. The fantasy in my head was that if it weren't for the industrial action, then all would be well. Chris's marriage and motherhood represented a woman fulfilled within the role carved out for her by the mining world she inhabited. I suppose, when you look upon strangers, you see what you want to see. And as a young female reporter in a still predominantly male world I wanted these women to be 'super-strong'. It made me feel good to think that here were my contemporaries, who hadn't been as fortunate as myself in some respects, but nonetheless had had the guts to take on a powerful government for the sake of their families; their home-lives stitched together with love and loyalty. As I write this, with the benefit of history and hindsight, I see my own naivety. Quite a different reality was taking place in many homes.

Relationships were under terminal pressure, but the faint cries of dying loves were drowned out by the roar of the picket lines.

When we finally sat down for a chat I realised how stupid I had been to make shallow assumptions. Not that Chris would have confided in me twenty years ago, nor that it would have occurred to me to ask too deeply how things were in her marital bed. To win some degree of trust from people in the mining communities at that time was tricky, because of the dislike of journalists. So, having persuaded someone to talk, then to launch in with questions about how her marriage was holding up was not an option – or so I thought. Perhaps Chris would have opened up then, but I suspect not. From what she told me, the split hurt like hell, and plunged her life and that of her two children into temporary chaos. She could discuss it freely now as twenty years was plenty of time to get over a failed marriage.

I learned there was much behind her upbeat exterior. Her life was punctuated with violence and it had nothing to do with clashes on the picket lines. If anything, the dispute had worked in her favour. It provided her with a much-needed escape route, and the courage to take it.

Chris lived in Hoyland – not my favourite former mining town – in the Dearne Valley. It wasn't far from where my family used to live, and it held no fond memories for me. It was one of those places where my mental picture was of a colourless townscape with no heart nor hope. There are those who love it, and will be outraged by my point of view – but that is all it is, a point of view. I am certain there is plenty of history in the stones and mortar of the area, and when the sun shone, which it must do from time to time, it would have cheered things up a bit. But I'm sorry to say that to me it was a grim corner of the world, without sunlight or cheer. This image wasn't improved as I drove to Chris's house, with the rain coming down so heavily that I had to put my windscreen-wipers on extra-fast.

I shuddered to think that this, too, might have been my fate; that the sickly greyness could have been my lifetime companion. It was a thought that made me struggle to breathe. I felt grateful that this was not my reality, nor my children's. I saw no charm in the drab houses that stood shoulder-to-shoulder, the streets full of men who had smoked themselves old. It is an almost irrational dislike that I had for the area, I suspect, because it represented what I had escaped from in my youth. Alongside this very personal aversion was an admiration for those who persevered and made a life out of such poor raw material.

Chris had a semi-detached house. They all looked pretty much the same from the road – pebble-dash façades squatting behind little front gardens with tufts of determined grass. There was an assortment of fences and gates and paths. Among the neighbouring houses, the windows were dressed with net curtains that twitched as my car pulled up outside. Women in these houses were known for 'wearing out the windows', which meant they were forever peering out of them into the world beyond their domestic authority. The homes were nondescript – rows and rows of them clustered all over the area like the houses you see inhabiting a military compound, built uniformly for a definite purpose, each house made to provide cover, security and warmth, nothing more. It was under that ethos that they were put up for miners and their families. What was different now was that miners no longer inhabited them. The bricks and mortar remained, but with new families in occupation, people who had moved in knowing only vaguely, if at all, of the history that had been played out in and around their four walls.

The actual look of the place hadn't changed much. When I poked my nose out of the car, I recognised immediately the smell in the air. It was the nostril-stinging odour of burning coal. Looking up, I could see wisps of dark smoke wriggling out of chimneys, which struck me as a bit odd because it was June and was technically quite warm outside, although the rain did play to the feeling of chilliness. Perhaps the comfort of coal was necessary, whatever the weather. At least the grates remained true to their heritage – although the coal they were burning was probably cheap stuff shipped in from another country. It was only possible to grasp the true character of these houses when you got past the front door. It was inside where people had made their mark; the exteriors kept you guessing.

It took Chris time to come to the door. When she opened it I realised the delay was because she was struggling to move quickly and was having to rely heavily on a walking stick. Her body was bent and a bit twisted. A pang of sympathy stirred inside me, though it was quickly snuffed out by Chris, who seemed to read my mind and was not going to allow me to pity her. She told me to take no notice of the stick and that most days she got about just fine. She made it clear that she had the disease under control. With a chronic, debilitating illness, you either let it rule you or you it; in her case Chris was the boss. Chris's living-room was stacked with boxes – her son David, who was twenty-five, was moving his stuff out. In the midst of the packing cases was a tiny kitten called Red scrabbling among the cardboard, full of naughtiness and cheek – a bit like Chris back in the eighties. The name reflected Chris's politics.

It came as a surprise to find her using a walking stick to move around. I know that sounds stupid; she had told me about the MS on the phone, but my image of her was a postcard from twenty years ago. Marching along at the head of the crowd, head held high, shoulders back, with an air of childlike excitement. The picture used on the front cover of this book shows Chris on the extreme right. She was always the first to volunteer for a bit of demonstrating or picketing, young and exuberant. To her it was more of a laugh than anything else. She says the police would often chase her, but she always gave them the slip because she was too quick for them. She also knew her way around much better, so she could duck out of their way.

Actually, as we began to talk about the past and mentally stepped back in time, the walking stick disappeared somehow. It was put to one side as Chris sat on her couch and spoke animatedly, waving her arms around and laughing. We can't change time, but time does change us; it's just that we prefer not to notice it. In my head I am still a fresh-faced girl of twenty-four; like the walking stick, the lines vanish when I am distracted by tales of my youth.

Chris made us some tea. I didn't help, despite the fact that she struggled with the stick, sugar, teabags, kettle and so on. I felt she wouldn't have welcomed a fuss; clucking around her offering to do this or that would have been more of an annoyance than anything else.

As we settled down in the living-room with the bundle of fur rampaging around in the background, Chris launched straight into the nightmare of her marriage – she left the pussyfooting to the kitten.

No bloody wonder I ended up with MS when you think about stuff I got up to and the stress from strike. Me marriage ended during it. My husband had an affair in strike. I divorced him as soon as we come out of it.

I wasn't ready for her bluntness, and was even more surprised when she told me her husband could be physically aggressive. They were married for almost ten years. From early on, Chris said he would go out drinking, either with or without her, then come home, and there would be volatile confrontations. She tried to say this without showing any emotion, but it was

147

impossible for her completely to hide the pain she felt, remembering those distressing times. Chris, who was a teenager when she married, was a spirited young woman. She was a fighter, so she would answer him back and refuse to do as she was told. This invariably led to conflict. He was 6ft tall and strong, and worked down the pit as a ropeman – a job that entailed securing huge ropes.

Gradually her spark began to go out. She said she felt crushed under the weight of an unhappy marriage. She was treated as though she wasn't valued and therefore began to believe she was worthless. Chris's husband was a flying picket. He would go off most nights with the other men. What the men and their families knew was that, as well as picketing, he was seeing a woman in Nottinghamshire. In that close environment it would have been hard to disguise the truth among the pickets. As often happens in these cases, everyone but those most closely affected knew about it; Chris didn't have a clue at first. Gradually, though, her friends and neighbours started to let her know. It is hard to be a messenger when the news is so unpleasant.

It were somebody at Nottingham he were knocking off. I sent a private detective after him, 'cos, thing were, I were doing so much for strike I were so busy. Even people that knew him come back and said you ought to know what's going on. 'Course it were shit that – I were putting meself out and putting me kids out for strike and that's what he were up to. She were actually single, but obviously we were busy down that area because that's where all scabs were to start with, wasn't it, till they started infiltrating everywhere else?

She did me a favour at end of day, to be quite honest with you. That year, 'cos we were both doing our own thing, that entirely separated us anyway, so I think even if he hadn't have done that, I'd have still divorced him because I couldn't have

148

gone back to doing what I were doing, being stuck at home with two kids and him being as he was.

There were always more trouble when he'd been to pub. If I think about it, strike put me back to what I were before, because our Ruth, me young sister, would say to me, 'Why don't you just keep your mouth shut? Why do you have to answer him back?' It were because he's not my gaffer, sort of thing, and she'd say, 'But Christine, you know what's going to happen.' I did know, but end of day I've still got to say what I've got to say, so I suppose in a way that's how I were. I had that knocked out of me, and then strike sort of give it me back, if you know what I mean. I stood upon my own two feet again.

It were actually just before strike ended that I told him he had to leave, and you know you can see that look. I started cleaning me nails – you know like you do when you're nervous and that. It were where we used to live up road here, and he says, 'Oh aye, where you gonna send divorce papers?' So I recited the address of woman he was seeing and you should have seen the look on his face. It were worth all them years, it really were, because he just never thought that I would do that. He'd had other affairs as well, like. So next thing table went up in air, chairs went flying, and he come round and he did get hold of me.

I'd got these scissors in me hand and I just stuck em in here [motioning as if to his shoulder] there like that, and I thought one of us has got to let go here, and I thought no, I'm not. Well, he did back off and that were it. I weren't backing down then, and he knew as well, and he just packed up and went. He went that afternoon.

You'd obviously changed enough in that period of time to stand up to him.

Yeah, I weren't having it, not any more. I couldn't have gone back to live that life.

And how old were you when you married him?

149

I were 17. He were eight years older than me. I were talking to a fella about six month ago, and he were like part of couple that we used to knock about with when we were younger, like. They were older than us. He says to me, 'You're not with him any more, are you?' I says, 'No, I'm not.' He went, 'You were just a bud when he picked you from that tree, and he ruined yer.' And I thought, so people did know things, they never said owt but they knew, didn't they?

The way our marriage was did change me in a lot of ways, because as I say, you find you're walking round dragging your feet and your head's down there all the time, and then strike, well that sort of got me back up there. But I think it did spoil me for relationships in future, though, because you don't tolerate idiots either. You know, yeah, I'm still on me own. I've had a couple of long-term relationships, but I'm not bothered. I'm forty-six now. I'm not cooking and cleaning for anybody. I wouldn't mind somebody just for weekends – that'll be alright.

It's like now, when you see programmes about this on telly and you say, 'Just leave him, just leave him,' and then I think, you were same Christine, and you didn't. Because they erode your confidence altogether; it's like you don't know who you are, what you're there for; you've no confidence. You think, 'Oh, nobody would look at me. Who'd want me?' 'cos that were like when I first got divorced, it were 'Oh, who's going to be bothered? – I'm stuck on me own with two kids.' But I were wrong; I had time of me bloody life, me.

Did you? They were queuing round the block?

Near enough. Oh, you know what it's like, they'd be thinking, 'She's just got divorced, she must be gagging for it.' Especially all married men. I've had one of them, and I've got rid of him.

And were you gagging for it?

Were I bloody hell! I weren't bothered. Bloody male arrogance isn't it, at end of day. You know, they think we can't survive without them.

150

A key factor in how Chris changed during the year-long strike was realising that she wasn't alone. Yes, she had her family, she was one of six children; but it was teaming up with other women like herself that made her see she didn't have to submit to a life where each day dragged her down. When people are subjected to repeated aggression they shut off to the world around them. They withdraw into themselves, where they can feel safer. They become wrapped up in the cotton-wool of their minds for self-protection. Chris was stuck in a downward spiral. How ironic that it took a destructive event like the strike of 1984/85 to free her from a domestic asphyxiation. The death of the pits was her resurrection.

Chris became heavily involved with picketing and running one of the largest soup kitchens in the area. Although she was young, she found that people would do as she asked; she discovered leadership skills that would be put to good use in the years to come. The soup kitchen was set up in a nightclub called The Birdcage. Chris says it burned down a few years ago, but at the time they were grateful that it was made available to the mining families, even though the kitchen was no bigger than one you would find in a small terraced house. The local Labour Party donated a cooker, and the owner of the club rewired half the kitchen to get it working.

The women held a market stall in town and raised the princely sum of £37 to get started. That was only the beginning; with local press coverage and word of mouth, people began making personal donations to the kitchen, especially pensioners, many of whom were retired miners or their wives, so they could sympathise with the next generation. The kitchen was a great success. The mood among the people was to pull together in this fight for the pits, so there were plenty of volunteers. There were so many women offering to help at The Birdcage, the organisers managed to put together a fortnightly rota so no one had to work there for too long. This was important, as the women were having to juggle the rest of their lives to make time to help out.

We were only one that were open five days at Birdcage at Elsecar; it were local nightclub then. I mean, that's been burnt down since, nowt to do with us like; but yeah, we were only one that were open five days a week. Obviously it took hours, didn't it, 'cos we used to do about three sittings as well, so it were, like, continual people in and out all time. So we started down there at 9 o'clock in morning, and Keith, my mate's husband, used to nip us up to fetch kids from school at half past three, and then we'd have to go down and finish off, for clearing up and everything like that. It were like a full-time job. After that, come ten o'clock at night we'd be off somewhere else picketing, then back two or three o'clock in morning. When you think about hours that we kept, we ought to be worse off than we are.

Me ex-husband's cousin used to give us a sack of beefburgers and a sack of sausages. They were really good round here for our food kitchen, they really were good, except for chip 'ole [fish-and-chip shop] man – he wanted to charge me for tatties. Well, our MP went down to talk to him and tell him we weren't gonna pay it. That were really cheeky, that were; I never went in that chip shop again. See, he weren't even from round here. I think that's what difference were, 'cos if he had have been a local lad he wouldn't have thought about charging.

The Birdcage was more than simply a place for people to eat. It served as an emotional support centre. People would come in, sometimes whole families, and chat to neighbours who they might previously have nodded to, but now were getting to know. It created a wartime spirit, where people came together through hardship. They would share their troubles, tales of picketing, and ideas about how to get by on the small amounts of benefit they were getting.

In a charity book published by Barnsley WAPC during the strike, Chris wrote about the kitchen. She said she had seen great changes in people as a result of the centre opening its doors. For instance, she wrote about older men who weren't usually bothered with children, actually nursing them while their parents ate their meal in peace. It was centres like this that kept up morale.

I remember going to London to different demos; I used to arrange coaches from here. I spoke in House of Commons once, asking for money. I were really nervous, and I were stammering and that, and they started clapping me to encourage me. I'm sure one of lasses would have that written down somewhere, whoever were taking notes. Actually it might have been them at Barnsley WAPC that put me forward to do it. What I had to do were talk about how it were affecting us, and I were asking for money for food kitchen; it were for donations for food kitchen that we wanted.
And had you ever addressed a meeting like that?
Had I heck! God no. It were petrifying, it really was. I can remember I were really, really scared; me mouth were right dry.

Then Chris remembered she had a couple of plastic bags upstairs stuffed with bits and pieces from the strike. She thought the original might be in among that. Sure enough, when she brought the bags down we found her speech tangled up with WAPC T-shirts, and paperwork from the food kitchen.

The impact it had on Chris was profound. Discovering the ability to address such a powerful audience and be heard was a turning point. Chris says her family, especially her father, were proud of her for speaking out for her community and a way of life. It was a good feeling to have made a mark. Although at

153

the time she didn't realise the significance of her actions, she wasn't 'looking for medals', she was simply doing whatever she could to support the action. She believed totally in the fight for the men's jobs; never once did she doubt the rightness of the cause. Even today she says she would do it all again.

They were heady days. The voyage of discovery for Chris was exciting and stimulating. For the first time in her life she felt in control of her destiny. She had found a new self and she liked her. As the months went by, she realised that her life had changed forever, although she couldn't grasp how all-encompassing that change was.

In the BWAPC book, Chris wrote:

After the strike we will have to find somewhere to channel our energy, most of us will never be able to sit at home again. We, as women, have realised the power we have to do something like this and keep it going, day after day. If someone had said six months ago that we could do something like this we'd have laughed in their faces. It's marvellous what mutual hardship can bring out in people. In a funny sort of way, we have a lot to thank the strike for. We have emerged stronger and more determined as people and we are strengthened as a community.

Today, she recalls:

At some point you start wondering, God, what am I gonna do after, when this is all over? Because you've that much to do and you're enjoying it. I think if everybody's honest, it gave you that little bit of power and all, which would be important to me from life I'd led. It were like, you can ask people to do things and they'll do it. You know, 'Oh, can you just do that and you just do that', and they say, 'Yeah, yeah, yeah.' You think, 'I like this'; it does change you, makes you more determined. You sit and think, could you go back to before? You know, get up and read paper in morning till it's time to pick kids up from school. You just realise that you were doing nowt before. Although I've always worked in a way, but that made you realise you're not really working, you're not really doing owt, you're not really living.

You're talking a year, near enough, where you were fully occupied all them hours a day doing what you were doing. I mean, coming back home at two o'clock in morning, soaked through to skin; get in bed 'cos you got to be back up again in morning. You just carried on. I think we could have kept that up for years and years, to be quite honest with you, 'cos spirit just got stronger and stronger. In end, as more people were going back to pit, I know people were thinking, it's forgone conclusion, but there's still that hard core there that still won't give up; while ever we were out, we were out, and that were it. *There must have been a part of you that'd be quite scared about letting go of it.*

Yeah, 'cos like I say, what are you going to go back to? What are you going to do after that? I knew I weren't going to go back to married life, no way; but then, God, I'm on me own with two kids. What am I going to do? Then August 1985 I got a job, and were working, and never looked back. I went through all that and brought up two kids on me own and all. I know I ended up with MS, but then there's people who ends up with worse. You do make best of bad deal and you'd no choice. I don't know what union would have come up with next, but they wouldn't have won it at end of day; but that time we 100 per cent believed it, and that's why we fought for it, you know. And probably if situation were same again, we'd do same again, definitely.

Some of the things that went on were laughable. Like a mate of mine that got arrested. She was about my size. She was supposed to have spotted police about half a mile up a hill, run down this hill, got to bottom, uprooted a lamp-post and formed a barricade. And all this before police got down. Well, to do that on her own she must have been really strong. She was a councillor's wife and she were brilliant. She was charged, but it were dropped after strike. Or you'd have three people on a street corner and you were done for rioting. You see things that go off on telly these days and you think, why don't you bring those rules back that you had for us?

I never got in trouble. I could run fast then, say, I used to get away, like, 'cos like you could nip up through park and everything. Police were all from Met. Well, they weren't even coppers, half of them, let's face it, not with trousers halfway up their legs. No, we were scuppered right, weren't we. Army blokes and that, weren't they? I sometimes think back and really, in a way you've got to take you're hat off to Thatcher, because she knew what she were doing. I still wouldn't have voted for her, though.

At the time of the strike, Chris's children were only little – David was five and Kerry three. She says her son was old enough still to have memories of the strike. He got caught up in the drama and anger of the dispute; there aren't many five-year-olds who would know what a 'scab' was, but David did. Typical of mining communities, Chris still regards those who returned to work as lepers. She says it was tantamount to being convicted of murder; no one would forget or forgive. Recently she saw the man who was the first to go back to work at Cortonwood colliery. She was outraged that he tried to talk to her. It is a legacy of anger that shows no signs of dying down with time.

My son David says he can remember standing on steps at top of food kitchen shouting 'scabs' at bus going downhill.
Scabs at five?
Weren't we awful, bringing us kids up like that? But David is a bit of a loyal person, so I wonder if that had any bearing on how he looked at things, you know – other people you're

supposed to trust let you down. There's always got to be some lasting after-effects, haven't there, you know. But sometimes I think about scabs, yeah, some ways it might be easier to forgive and forget and let it go and that, but then I think no, 'cos it affected an important part of our life, our jobs.

Having links with the kitchen helped keep the family fed. Chris says they were fortunate that in her area they did get some help from the social services.

We didn't have to pay us rent, it were paid by social. I know that didn't work for everybody. Gas and electric I can't remember, we were all electric up there, 'cos that were different house to this one, 'cos we ate every day at food kitchen anyway, and we did a proper dinner. It were chips, meat and veg, or tatties, meat and veg; you didn't just go down and get a sandwich and that. A lot of time if I were busy my two kids would be with my sisters, so they'd be feeding them not me, if you see what I mean. So maybe if I hadn't been so busy I would have found it were really, really hard. He were never here, obviously, 'cos he were off picketing or whatever.
What did you think you took with you from the strike?
For me personally, self-confidence, pride, that I am gonna stand me ground, you know, you're not gonna get me down ever again. If I've got something to fight for I'm going to fight for it, if I believe in it enough that's what I'm going to do. You know, it just changed everybody's outlook I think, and you'd got so many more friends and it definitely brought people together, definitely. Like I say, them women that we were working with together in food kitchen, I've actually babysat for their children, like when I were younger. It's a leveller, like I were probably twenty year younger than most of them, but I'd say to 'em, 'Can you do this or that?' and they'd say, 'Yeah, no problem'. We pulled together, and it were great.

157

Has that spirit lasted twenty years?

I'd say not, because obviously a lot of people moved away after pits closed. They follow work, don't they? For long enough Elsecar were like a ghost town. Anyway, now you can't buy a house in area; you just can't get one for people wanting to move there.

When the strike ended, Chris had to rebuild her life. Her time on the front line had given her a thirst for living. For the first time she had an ambition – to keep going and not to go back to the way things were before. Despite the buzz of rediscovering herself, the end of the dispute meant she had her work cut out, as she had no husband, two young children, no income and no savings. But she was fired up. The new talents she'd discovered would be put to good use – in particular the realisation that she could survive and thrive in a male environment. It had also been a revelation to her that she could give orders and people did as she said. Going into management had never been something she had considered in the past, but it was to be in the future.

Chris had always been clever. At school she was one of those pupils who never had to do any work and still got good marks in her exams. Much to the regret of her headmistress, Chris left school at sixteen to work in a sewing factory.

I know this sounds big-headed when you say it like, but I never really needed to go to school, if you know what I mean. Like me secondary school I wagged it for about three year and passed all me GCSEs. But some people are like that aren't they? But me Mum were clever, and me Dad. I went to King Street School, which were a good school. We used to win all music concerts and that, regular. I liked that place, but in secondary it got boring, and that's really why I started wagging it, 'cos they weren't telling me nowt, you know – they didn't keep your interest.

What were you doing when you were wagging it? What were you up to?

We used to go rec and smoke or . . . actually, one of me mates used to live at end of this street here, you know, whose parents were working. They'd be houses we'd go to, in fourth year. I used to go, 'cos I were actually going out with David fourth to fifth year and I used to go to work with him, but I did go back for me exams. When I left, headmistress wrote across bottom of my report, 'What a waste.' You see, thing is ours is a family of six so it's not just me they were interested in, so you know, there were like five others that Mum and Dad were looking after, and they were both working full-time, so I suppose you do get overlooked a bit, don't you? I were fourth from eldest; I've two sisters and a brother older than me, and then two sisters younger.

Do you remember, did you have any ambitions or anything?

No, I don't think we did then, 'cos jobs were easy to come by as well at that time. I mean, I had two jobs lined up before I even left school, but they were both sewing factories. I could use a sewing machine because me mum had taught us that, 'cos me mum used to make all us clothes. I suppose it were just a natural progression to go to something that you knew; lads went to pit, girls all went to a factory. It would be different in this day and age, but then that's how it were. I earned bloody good money though, while I were in factory. I was a fast worker and I did piece-work.

Although finding work after the strike was difficult, Chris did get a job at a local company that supplied dry and frozen goods to large shops. She started off working with her sister, sorting teabags at a firm called J. Marren Ltd. Chris learned how to drive a forklift truck, and was better at it than any of the men. She rapidly moved on to take a managerial role. Having entered a man's world, she had the confidence to take command – the tables had turned. She was telling the men what to do, and if they didn't she would come down hard on them, threatening them with the sack. She was given the job of foreman and showed that a woman could be just as effective as a man, and every bit as tough. She laughs now, because apparently a lot of the men were terrified of her. Chris not only matched them, she became their boss.

The work started off in August '85. Me and me sister were stripping teabags out of one and putting them in plain bags; and then I were supervisor. Then I got all me qualifications for forklift driving and counterbalance on sidewinder – yeah, I had both of them – and I were only one that got 95 per cent on pass rate on fork-lift test an all. Then I were like foreman, running warehouse and cold store. I had all men answerable to me. I were there until '96, when MS got too bad for working.
The strike, I suppose, in the long run did you a favour really?

It did, it did me a big favour. I stood on me own two feet then, and that were that, it were. Before that I couldn't have gone and done that job up there, you know, telling boss what it were all about, telling them what to do. And I had that as well, taking no bleeding notice of a chuffing woman – what's she know? I'd say, 'I went through harder bloody training and did more shit jobs than you've done to get where I am, so you can either do what I did or you can find somewhere else.'
And they did it?

Yeah, oh yeah. Although I did not have anybody walk off. In fact, I only ever had to sack one, and he just thought he were going to stand about all day. Since I've left and have been drinking locally, they say, 'God I were terrified of you when I worked there.' 'Why, what were there to be scared of? All I wanted you to do was do your job.' So even, like, now I'm still, like, 'If you'd have done as you were told, we wouldn't have had a problem.' So I suppose its made me a bit more bolshy.

Without the experience of strike, I wouldn't have been able to say, 'Oh well, I'll go and run a factory', or owt like. I didn't know if I'd go back to work, 'cos I still had two kids. I got one daughter under school age. Jobs I'd done from having her were like sewing at home, or part-time jobs and that.

Chris was forced to give up her job in 1996 because the MS was getting worse. She says things in her life go in cycles; she is preparing for whatever life throws at her next. The MS is taking its toll, but Chris refuses to give in to it.

I'll never go back to work, because I'll never be fit enough, like. I mean, I'm alright a short distance using that crutch. I don't know if, long-term, this beta interferon might improve owt, but I do physiotherapy as well. But over last three years me walking ain't improved.

I've been through that first stage, remission/relapsing. I'm in secondary progressive now. If I hit chronic progressive, they say it'll be two years, and I'll be in a wheelchair and no good to man or beast, like. But as I said, when it gets to that, that's when I'll be popping off, like; I'm not asking anybody to help me, I'll do it myself like. It might not come to that, 'cos I'm sure we'll get a cure in my lifetime; I am sure it's possible, 'cos if they give me something now to stop my relapses, which, touch wood, its over two years since I had one, and I were having four a year, so you've got a good reason to keep hoping.

There's people that's, like, got what I've got and they're not like me at all. I have me down times, like, but you'll not see it; nobody would see it, 'cos it's so brief. I think, well, there's worse than you love. But there is, isn't there?

Surprisingly, one thing that has come out of Chris's illness is a better post-marital relationship with her ex-husband, whose

161

marriage to the woman from Nottingham broke down. As I said at the beginning of this chapter, two decades is plenty of time to get over a bad marriage, even, it seems, such a volatile one. Chris says that he had just been staying at her house for the first time – in the spare bedroom. He had brought their daughter Kerry up, who went to live with him in London when she was sixteen. Chris could see no reason not to let him stay. It is hard to be angry for all those years, and the one thing she did stress was that she would not criticise him as a dad. Although he moved to London, he would still help out with the kids, sending money if it was needed. He took them on holidays; he and his new wife would have them for weekends, which gave Chris time to herself, or to spend with her toyboy.

As mobility is such an issue with Chris, she wanted an automatic car to help her get around. Her ex-husband loaned her money to help buy one. It was only £400, but it made quite a difference to Chris.

I think, what with me having kids – 'cos obviously from '85 I brought 'em up on me own, 'cos he moved down London, where he still is. He's actually just been here for a few days, 'cos our Kerry's been up; he were supposed to be bringing her up on Tuesday night. Last year he paid me for that car. I says to our David, 'Ask your dad if he'll loan me some money, 'cos I need a new car, automatic like.' And I knew he'd just got a pension payout, and I think legally I were entitled to some of that anyway, so I says, 'Ask your dad'. It were sneaky how I did it, if I can borrow money for car. It were only £850, so he says, 'Tell your mum just to put £400 of it back, and I'll stand other half.' So I says to our David, 'That's a bit.' He went, 'Mother, take it!' I says, 'Yeah, but what's come back on it?' So all time then, I'm thinking, and then later on I sent him a text, 'I'm gonna put another £200 back in your account, you know, for car.' He went, 'Don't bother, just leave it.' So I've had that eighteen month now.

When he came up, it were first time he's stopped, but it were only because we asked him to bring Kerry up, 'cos trains were supposed to be on strike last Tuesday. So when the strike were called off, I says, 'What about your dad?' She says, 'He still wants to come up with me if it's alright.' I says, 'Well, fair enough.' Kerry slept with me, 'cos we've got three bedrooms, and every day I kept thinking, they're going home today, and then on Friday, Kerry says, 'What you gonna be doing then today?' He says, 'Well, I might as well hang on now and take you home in morning, hadn't I?'

What was he like? Was it the first time you'd seen him in a while?

Well, I've spoken to him and that, obviously, because we've still got kids between us. I can't knock him for being a good dad, never. Because even when I got MS I'd be off three month at a time. So if I rung up and said kids needed something, there'd be £50 straight in post, no questions asked. He's taken 'em abroad three times – they've been to Africa and Turkey.

It did get to point where I had to tell kids actually why I got divorced, but I didn't want to influence them one way or another, so they were fifteen before I told them. It would have been too easy to tell 'em when they were kids, and it were possible that then they wouldn't have wanted to go to him and, to be fair, he used to pick 'em on Friday; I'd got all weekend to myself then. There were him and her stuck at home babysitting – well that was fine by me. More ways of skinning a cat, isn't there?

Chris has a knack of having the last laugh, no matter how bad things have been. She has the ability to see things in a positive light. Even with her secondary-stage MS, she has a belief that it can be beaten. She also has the ability to surprise you. For example, one thing I wasn't expecting from this level-

headed lady was that she had a lot of faith in fortune-telling.
She has regularly had her tarot cards read by the same woman
since the end of the strike. What must have started out as a
laugh became more serious when the woman's predictions
proved to be accurate. Whether you believe in it or not, I do
think fortune-telling is a kind of therapy in itself. Think of it
this way: you pay someone to listen and discuss intimate
details of your life. Generally, they have nothing else to do
with you, so there is no axe to grind, no relationship politics at
stake. So you can allow yourself time to think and talk about
your needs, hopes and desires. It is an opportunity to examine
your life without derision or criticism. It doesn't feel like
therapy as it can be disguised as a bit of fun. For Chris, it
seems to have helped bolster her through the darkest of times;
and made her look to the future rather than hang on to a
painful past. She is the 'eternal optimist'.

Funny thing is, with me, you know, main events in my life seem
to go in nine-and-a-half year cycles, like, me marriage ended
after nine-and-a-half year, I left work after nine-and-a-half year,
and I'm at nine-and-a-half years now, so I wonder what's going
to happen. You see, I'm ever optimistic.
I like to have me cards read. You're either into that thing or
you're not. I've been to same woman since 1985/6. She thinks
I'm going to go into something like what she's doing. She told
me to start going to spiritualist church. She says that's where I
ought to start. She's never told me a thing wrong in all them
years. I were just divorcing Dave when I started seeing her.
First off she told me about two babies that I hadn't had and
two children I did have. She said you've recently got divorced,
and he's regretting it big-time; at some time he'll try to come
back, which he did once.
    There were all sorts of things, like; one were really scary.
Three year ago she says to me, 'Yer dad's still with us?' I says

yeah, but I knew, she didn't actually say he's gonna die. 'Well just keep your eye on him, because he's been a bit too quiet, and that's not like yer dad.' A while later I went down to me daughter's at Hertford, and me sister rung me up. She says me dad's gone into hospital. I knew he weren't gonna come back out. It's like, you know how you get that right strong feeling and you know you're right? And he didn't, he never come out.

Chris's card reader told her that, despite her illness, she still had something important to do. Chris shared that view; she didn't know what it was going to be, but she knew life had something more in store for her. As she spoke about her future it was possible to see that the spirit that had taken her so far was still evident. Perhaps she will write as other women in her situation have done. It's hard to know where the next chapter will take Chris, but I will be watching with interest.

CHAPTER SIX

A Sin With No Forgiveness: Jenny and Harry Evans

In one of the few books published just after the 1984/5 strike, there is a powerful picture of a crowd of pickets and their supporters at Cortonwood colliery, in Brampton. It was taken in February 1985 at the end of the dispute – a time when it was clear that the government had won. The world in which these people had lived was coming to an end; nothing would ever be the same. As the camera captured the moment, none of those in its eyeline knew what tomorrow held. One thing was certain, though – the men were faced with the ignominy of returning to work, having been crushed by the powers that be. All the hardship, rage and fury hung in the air on that freezing winter's day. The image was particularly poignant because Cortonwood was the pit where the strike began.

The three central characters in the shot are Jenny and Harry Evans with their daughter Marie, who was just a toddler at the time, but in the preceding months had become a familiar little face on the picket line at the pit. Harry, known as Nugger to his mates, was and is a union man to his marrow. Jenny has stood beside him throughout. In the photograph Harry is a picture of loss and despair, the suffering of the past twelve months etched on a face that looks as though it has gone ten rounds with Mike Tyson. Jenny is busy keeping Marie distracted by pointing into the crowds. As ever, her look is one of calm determination. In their copy of the book, all the key figures in the dispute have signed the picture – including

Arthur and Anne Scargill, Mick McGahey and Peter Heathfield. Jenny and Harry were well known and respected in hard-line union circles for their unwavering support of the strike.

The cost to the community was to prove to be all that Scargill had predicted – Cortonwood was on his home patch. Nugger knew Arthur well. They went to the same school; at one point they even lived on the same street. Nugger wouldn't hear a bad word said about the man who predicted the end of the coalfields. Cortonwood closed not long after the end of the strike, followed by other pits in the locality, and the tertiary industries such as the coke works disappeared with them. The same look of pain crosses Nugger's face today as he talks of how the area became a wasteland with no jobs, no income and, worst of all, no hope. The change was not just a financial one. The death of the pits cut right into the heart of many families. The events of the year-long dispute left a permanent emotional scar. So it was in the Evans household.

Jenny and Harry come as a team – you don't get one without the other. That is the way it has been since they married in 1975. They are two sides of the same coin. As with the other women in this book, the strike had a profound effect on Jenny – it gave her new confidence to take on roles that would never have occurred to her prior to manning the picket lines. She became a public speaker, a school governor and a karate black belt and instructor. But instead of making her want to leave behind her traditional role as a wife and mother, it made her more content to work her new-found freedoms around the homelife she cherished. That isn't to say the Evans family weren't torn apart by the dispute, but it wasn't husband and wife who split up; it was a deep-rooted rift between siblings that did permanent damage. One of Nugger's brothers was a strike-breaker, a scab – a crime for which there was no forgiveness.

Jenny and Harry Evans speak their mind, no matter what the consequences. They are blunt and brash and straight to the point. I knew that if they didn't like me, then I wouldn't have got the time of day out of them. Life was black and white – there were those they welcomed into their home and then there was the rest of humanity. Fortunately, I fell into the former category. For whatever reason, Jenny and Harry thought I was okay – for a journalist, that is. I think it was because the reports I did with them and their neighbours twenty years ago focused on the terrible struggle of the families to survive during the strike – it was a story that few news organisations were telling. They followed my career as I went from BBC radio to TV and newsreading. In the turmoil of those months during the strike, I developed a connection with them, whereby I became a part, albeit small, of their lives. When I rang them a few years ago to catch up, they greeted me like an old friend. We had a common history born out of the strike. We had been in it together. Admittedly we were coming at it from different directions, but anyone who has been in a war will tell you that only those who were actually there would understand what they had been through.

When I was out in the first Gulf war, based in Bahrain, I got to know quite a number of the Tornado pilots who were flying off to face possible death over Iraq in early-morning sorties. We would all drink together in the plush bar of the Sheraton the night before, and then meet in the early dawn – they were off to drop bombs; my camera crew and I were there to film them, and then go and tell the world what we could about their mission. In those life-and-death situations you get to know people very well. So when we all demobbed and came home some of them would call me to talk about events in the Gulf because no one in their family understood what had gone on. They needed to speak to someone who had shared a unique and dangerous experience.

My relationship with the Evanses was along those lines, if you replace the scuds and fighter planes with batons and bricks. As fellow witnesses to history, we were members of a special club. You couldn't pretend that you knew what the strike felt like – you had to have been there. Jenny and Harry still lived in the same house where I first met them. Little had changed as I drove down their road past the rows of humble pit houses. Of course, the legions of riot-clad police had long gone, as had the miners who had fled down these roads, ducking into the houses to escape arrest.

Inside, things had kept up with the fashion of the day. The grey walls, from my memory, were now brightly coloured; a huge TV babbled with the Tellytubbies to entertain the grand-children. The couple had made space for a new generation of their family by knocking down walls to create a large kitchen/diner. It was a comfortable, lived-in family home.

Another thing that had changed was the value of the property. Once these were homes that you couldn't give away, built in a utilitarian way by the Coal Board for their workers, two-up, two-down, and a bathroom. But in recent years the gentrification of the surrounding area and the influx of young families looking for affordable homes meant that prices were shooting up. Much to Nugger's delight, he'd been offered over £100,000 for the place – the main attraction was their large back garden. He chuckled as he told the story of a local man who had tried to offer him less than that for the place, and he'd been told to bugger off. This king wasn't moving from his castle. He just wanted to sit back and enjoy the windfall. I couldn't help but feel the irony that this good fortune was the long-term product of Thatcher's monetarist policies, which had fuelled the property boom. I didn't say as much, though – it wasn't the done thing to mention her name in this house. It would have been a bit like saying 'Voldemort' or 'He whose name cannot be spoken' in the Harry Potter books – it would have caused a sharp intake of breath and resurrected deep hatreds that were best left buried.

Their children, Marie and Neil, had grown up and left home, but the house still felt full of children. Their place had been taken by Marie's two little ones – Chloe and baby Olivia. Jenny and Harry had become grandparents and babysitters to the next generation of their family. Part of their relationship was to tease each other continuously. When I asked where Marie was working, Jenny told me she was a telephonist. Nugger chipped in that she was at Ventura. Jenny said, in a derisory tone, 'Now how the hell would she know what Ventura were? You don't know what it is, do you Triona?' 'Ay she does know, don't you Triona, you know what Ventura is? Tell her you do.' Risking a minor world war, I hazarded a guess that it was a call centre – which was almost right, and triggered a little more barbed banter between the two. It ended with boisterous laughter, as did all their clashes.

Jenny is a slender, attractive woman. Although she has a small frame, there is nothing lightweight about her. At school she loved sport, but it wasn't until after she had her children, and after the 1984/5 strike, that she realised her ambition to compete internationally as a blackbelt in karate. I have never seen her wear make-up; she doesn't need any. Nugger is fond of talking about how Jenny was a great 'catch' thirty years ago when they married. You don't need to prompt him much to get him to regale you with tales of jealousy among his contemporaries that he had won the heart of this lass, who was the daughter of a local celebrity – a FIFA referee. Jenny just laughs it off, saying she could still have her pick if she wanted – saying she might yet, with a wink at me.

I recall how she would be down at the Alamo – the nickname for the wooden hut on the picket line at Cortonwood – with Marie, who was about two years old at the time. Jenny's big, dark eyes would stare out at events going on around her. Despite her diminutive size, you couldn't miss her in among the beefy miners, as she could shout and swear as loud and as furiously as any of the men.

It isn't easy to interview Jenny because Nugger is keen to have his say. When I asked, 'Did the strike change you?', Nugger, who was sitting at the other end of the kitchen playing with baby Olivia, piped up, 'Do you mean me, lass? Ah well of course it did . . .' Jenny turned to him and said, 'No, she means me, you silly beggar.' And so it went on. They had a rhythm all their own and trying to interrupt it was useless. Fortunately for me, a lifetime of putting Nugger back in his box meant that Jenny got the upper hand.

The strike made me go out more. It's not as if he said, 'You're stopping in', but if I thought, 'I'm going out', I would. I even got to become a governor at school. I wouldn't have ever dreamt of that in a million years. I wouldn't have thought I could ever speak in front of people. I got to the point of being a bit nervous of speaking in front of parents. And I thought, I'm getting really nervous here, and then I thought to myself, how can you be nervous when you used to make all row at picket line, and bit by bit it wore off and I stuck it out as a governor.

I didn't talk at the big rallies, but I did when different women were going round and they would ask us to speak. If one or two spoke, I were one of 'em. The worst time was after court, when we were at Sheffield and they were trying to free a load of men who'd been arrested on picket line. When me and me mate Christine went, we all had to go to this hotel after the case. They'd won and the men were all going free. There was great relief, as they'd been in for ten days. We had to go to this hotel, and there were the likes of the barrister Mike Mansfield, and others like him. They were saying that one of us had to speak. So I am there saying, 'Don't come to me!' And they're saying its okay. But then one of 'em says, 'Come on', and I am holding my daughter Marie's hand, and I said, 'Where we going?' They said, 'Go on, you're speaking', and shoved me into this room. There were a man from every area – Yorkshire, Newcastle, Durham, Wales. They were officials, and Arthur Scargill were there as well, and other barristers and media. I were absolutely petrified. I wondered how I was going to keep standing, as my legs were like jelly.

At this point Harry interrupted – he had made a speech at their daughter's wedding. 'Yeah, I know about public speaking; it wo' nerve-racking talking at wedding . . .' Jenny slapped him down: 'It's not same, Nugger.' Harry grumbled and got on with looking after Olivia, who was hungry and tired.

I had spoken out onto cameras beforehand. But speaking out when there are two or three of you is one thing; doing it on your own is another. When it came for me to speak out and all press were there, I thought, I don't believe this, and they said 'Go on', and that were it. Our Marie was sat with barristers. I were really shaking; I held onto chairs because I felt I were falling. But I did it all same, and all the while I were thinking, 'You sod Christine, I'll kill ya!' Because she had got me into this in first place. I had never done anything like that before strike, but after it I knew I could do it, so I never worried too much about talking out again. It got less scary, like.

Jenny's father was Arthur Holland. He had been a Barnsley miner but was heavily involved in football and trained to be a referee. He left the pit to work as a ground-keeper and to pursue his career in soccer. He made it to the big time, refereeing the cup final between West Ham and Preston at Wembley in 1964 – the former winning 3–2. Jenny was nine at the time. He also refereed in Europe for FIFA. The medals he got from these historic matches have pride of place in Jenny and Harry's living room. Not surprisingly, sport was always something that interested Jenny, although becoming a mum took precedence over any ambitions she might have had. It was only when her son Neil took up karate that Jenny renewed her interest in sport. When she took him to the local club, she would get terribly restless waiting for him, so she decided to join in.

When I were little I were keen on all sports, but then as I grew up and got married I were more concerned about me kids. Then when me lad Neil were growing up, he sparked off watching karate on TV and he took a liking to it. I were thinking about bullying that had been going on at school and put two and two together. I naturally took him to a local class. While I were sat there waiting for him it were irritating me, so I ended up getting involved and doing it and I carried on.

I got to go abroad twice for European competitions – to West Germany and Holland. I were a blackbelt first dan in kick-boxing, and I did Twelve Nations and I came out third for Great Britain, and then I went to West Germany and did what's called a Tiger Twin, and it's between a European and a world title, and I did that . . . Out of twenty-two nations I got third again. That were '89, so well after strike.

Nugger confirmed with some pride that you didn't mess with Jenny once she got her black belt. He said he had to watch his step. Certainly, the karate would have come in handy on the picket line.

They nicknamed me Jenny Two Balls. When I were just learning, there was a move called an upper cut in boxing, and we call it a Bolo Rising to body. Well, sometimes when I were first learning I aimed a bit too low; that weren't my intention, but that was what was happening. And so men were going to cover up as I were catching 'em down there. Once I come to learn it, and I knew it right, it were ok. But then the men were still joking wi' me about that and I never lost the nickname. I haven't done karate for some time now, but there again I still remember it – especially that two balls move. We always had a joke about that, I enjoyed it. I never dreamed I would have got to be a black belt. I have competed with men and women, and with little 'uns, but just to show 'em not to be scared. They were really frightened by bullies.

I really got on well fighting men – not competing, as they wouldn't let me, but I did at us own gym. When we went round to a certain place where my instructor were getting taught, he says for them to let me fight with men. When I did fight 'em even the men were there took back in amazement. I'm not a big lass but it don't make a difference – its how the strokes go and where you hit 'em. Sometimes they beat me, but I beat 'em as well.

Jenny works as a cleaner for her former karate instructor, who has a pub/nightclub. And although she left the sports arena a few years ago, her reputation lives on, something she delights in.

I am only a cleaner but still, there again, I am there having me say if need be. Where I work is where my instructor is – like, he owns this nightclub or pub, and basically I just clean there. Sometimes, if it gets that bad there, he says at least we got you to put on door. He keeps warning men to watch out for me; he says to them, 'You'd better watch her,' and they say they wouldn't want to hurt me. Well, he laughs and says it's her hurting you that you'd better be worried about.

Even when he went away he asked me to mind club. I was there to instruct and look after place. The sod. Put me in a right stew. But I did it.

Jenny went off to put the baby to bed. Once she was out of the room Nugger leaned forward and in a conspiratorial tone told me that I was lucky to find him alive. He said that he was refusing to eat Jenny's cooking these days, as he was certain that she was trying to do away with him in order to get the life assurance money.

> I went to doctor other day and I says to him, 'Does tha know what me wife did other day? She had cooked me supper and I were eating it and I saw that she were reading, and it were me life insurance policy. Well, I pushed food away and told her, "Tha's not to cook for me again!"'

By now Jenny was back in the room with the baby, who had decided not to sleep after all. She laughed, saying it was true that she had been studying the policy, but only to check that the payments were being made – honest! Then Nugger told how he put a pillow over her face the other night in retaliation. This prompted more laughter from the pair. It was obviously a favourite joke between them. I couldn't stop myself from asking how long they had been married. Thirty years in 2005. Perhaps foolishly, I teased them about having a bit of a do to celebrate their 'pearl' wedding anniversary and wanted to know if I was going to get an invite. The response was along the lines of 'yeah, if we live that long!'

They were such a tight double act that it was impossible to prise them apart. Although Nugger mourned the closure of the pit, he had settled well into being at home with his wife and grandchildren. As he sat in his comfy chair wrestling with Olivia, trying to make her take her bottle in order to stop her crying, he looked healthy and relaxed. Despite the passage of twenty years, he looked a hundred times better than he did in the photograph taken during the strike. I had a secret bet with myself that if the pit was still around and reopened, there would be no way Harry would get in the cage that took the men hundreds of yards down to the coalface. He lamented the lost way of life, but he had benefited from its passing.

Behind the laughter and teasing, Jenny and Harry were two people who could be as hard as nails. With them you were either in or out: there was no grey area. The couple featured in a documentary I did for BBC Radio 4 in 2004 to mark twenty years since the strike. Their story was one of being betrayed by their nearest and dearest. It was an illustration of how deep those emotions were, and are still, felt. A lot of the feedback from the programme included a degree of shock at how the Evanses could not let go the past and forgive Harry's brother. But if you put that to the couple, they shrug and dismiss this view; if you lived in a mining community, you would understand and empathise with their tough line on this issue.

During the strike, Harry's brother Frank had gone back to work. He was a 'scab'. It is a word that is still spat out like a curse, hissed through clenched teeth. The perpetrator was treated like the living dead, there was no remission. This was the eighth deadly sin. It was a crime with a life sentence and no such thing as time off for good behaviour. The taint of having a relative who was a scab touched the whole family – they were guilty by association. Worse still, Frank had the same nickname as Harry – Nugger – so the chances of getting the two men mixed up were great. In light of that, it is possible to see why the scabs own families were the hardest on them. It was important to create as great a distance as possible between your close family and the scab, or you risked being tarred – literally – with the same brush. Although Frank was not her blood relative, Jenny's fury at his actions is still as fierce today as it was when she first heard the news that he was a strike breaker.

Frank only went back for a week or so, but his family never forgave him and the sins of the father were visited on the rest of the family. Frank's wife and children were also ostracised. Even when Frank died a few years ago, Jenny and Harry didn't go to the funeral; in fact, they didn't know about his death for some weeks. They heard about it when they were out shopping. No tears were shed. The hatred for such betrayal outlived the pits. When Jenny spoke of Frank her face went hard; her anger was so intense that I could feel it.

When Harry got phone call . . . telling him he'd gone in, I couldn't believe it to start with. Anyway, eventually it came clear that he had gone back and, so as far as I was concerned, he was dead. He was dead. And I know for Harry he was dead as well; and that was it. Once a scab, always a scab. Never forgive, and never, ever forget.

Harry had to report to the union that he'd gone back in; that he was a scab. They both had the same nickname – 'Nugger'. He had to report him in or else, as my house was on doorstep of Cortonwood, it would be 'Let's have that Nugger at *this* end', and we would have had windows smashed. No way. So he reported him. As far as I was concerned he wasn't a brother-in-law to me. He was dead in our lives.

When they were on about trying to get him out again, Frank phoned up. I didn't want to speak to him. But the Union, the Miner's Union, said to Nugger, 'This is a chance for you to get Frank out.' Fair enough, so I left it to them. So, when Frank came here for a meeting with Harry and Union, I got Marie and I went down to the Alamo [the strike hut put up outside Cortonwood Pit] and stopped at Alamo. I didn't tell anybody 'cos my windows would have been smashed and everyone would have come to house, so I couldn't say anything.

When he went in, we were all threatened. But once they knew that it wasn't *my* husband that had gone in, it wasn't a problem. But it is upsetting that you have a brother or brother-in-law who's a scab. They knew that we had nothing to do with it. Yes, we're relations, but we can't do anything about that. They knew my husband wasn't going in; he could walk out of this house with his head held high. My kids and I could back their father, no problem.

But Harry did manage to repair the situation and got Frank out again? He was only in a week or so wasn't he? As it was such a short spell, could you not forgive him 'cos he did make it right?

No. Once a scab, always a scab!

Even for a short time?

A short time. A day. Don't make no difference: once a scab, always a scab. Once you've gone in as a scab, that's it. You've broke it, you've done it.

What about the impact on his family? Including his children?

I don't know; never been in touch at all. After the strike we did see Frank and his wife in town. Frank said something to Harry, and Harry started back arguing. I walked away. Frank's wife Winnie walked away in a different direction and that was end. We've had nothing ever else to do with them. Never.

Have you seen her since?

Never. Harry did once point her out in a shop, but I didn't recognise her.

And is she dead for you as well?

I'm not happy, but I can't blame her; she didn't go in. She backed her husband. Her husband's her husband.

Would you have anything to do with her now?

Well, had nothing to do with her at all. Not happy about it, but she backed her husband, so I can understand that. But I backed all the miners up, altogether, not just my husband. She didn't, she just backed her husband; end of story.

But all these years on, couldn't you forgive her? Find it in your heart to get back together?

Well, she doesn't want to get back with us, so it's just a dead end; so I've not been bothered. She's not phoned or come or anything, so why should I? I'm not breaking my neck for anybody?

What about for your children and grandchildren? Could you not see a time when the family could get back together again?

Mine didn't really know Winnie and Frank – well, me son did, but me daughter didn't. She was very little and didn't know her. Grandchildren of course had nowt to do with it.

Is that the way you think it'll stay? That rift goes back to just a few days of scabbing?

Yeah. Yeah. It'll stand there. It'll stand there forever.

No going back?

No. No way.

So, in some ways, the sins of their father have been visited upon their children?

Yeah. When it was the strike in 1926, the ones who were scabs, the miners didn't talk to them, and it's still the same, whoever's still alive now. And it's the same now; this is how it goes. You can't just forget or forgive. If they'd hadn't gone back in, you don't know, more could have happened and we could have succeeded; if they'd stuck by one another. That's what you say, 'United We Stand'. And that's how I believed it. Frank were a scab. He were dead to us. And that was that.

For an outsider it is hard to comprehend this fierce anger and hatred that lives beyond the grave. Let me try and put it in context.

Frank's return to work put all his relations at risk of reprisals. It was just before Christmas, at the end of 1984, nine months into the strike. A few men had started to go back at pits across the country. Cortonwood, as the colliery where the strike began, had a particular significance; so when men started returning there, the push to get them to come out again was a matter of great importance to the NUM. The actions of Frank and a handful of other men at Cortonwood were seen to pose a serious threat to the future of the whole dispute. It showed weakness in the ranks of the miners and increased the likelihood that those men who were wavering would be tempted to join the strike breakers. As the festive season approached, families who were struggling to feed their children were faced with the prospect of having nothing to put on the Christmas table or under the tree for the kids. Psychologically, it was the worst time for men to break ranks. The trickle back to work was flagged up by the government as a sign that they were going to be victorious – a view echoed in the press at the time. And as we now know, it was only a matter of months before the NUM had to admit defeat. Today, the belief among many miners still holds that, if it weren't for the 'scabs', they could have kept the strike going and brought the government to its knees. Obviously, the miners had no crystal ball to tell them what the outcome was to be, so in November 1984 they believed it was all still to fight for. The imperative was to keep the strike going – that meant using whatever means they could to 'persuade' those who had gone back to work to rejoin the strike. It was crucial to the dispute's success that the miners stood together.

It's not surprising, then, that the 'scabs' were on the receiving end of a blind anger that had built up after months of hardship and frustration. The men who crossed the picket line were subjected to verbal and physical abuse, as were their wives and children. Their lives were made hell as the community closed ranks: their homes were vandalised, shops wouldn't sell them goods, pubs and clubs banned the men from coming in. They became social pariahs. Twenty years later, it wasn't easy to find men who had gone back to work who were prepared to speak about it. Incredibly, some still lived in the old mining communities where they were ostracised and isolated. Just mentioning that I was looking for a scab would alter the whole dynamic of a conversation.

In one of the pubs in Brampton, for instance, my colleague, BBC producer Jim Frank, and I got a warm welcome when we said we were doing a documentary about the strike. People gathered round and volunteered anecdotes and reminiscences by the dozen. It was drinks and joviality all round. There wasn't anything they wouldn't help us with, even calling friends to see if we could interview Mrs Such-and-Such or Mr So-and-So . . . But when I asked if they knew where any of the 'scabs' lived, the mood took a definite downturn. People rolled their eyes and became vague. It was as though a chill wind had blown into the pub and suddenly we were outsiders. As they prevaricated I felt certain they knew names and addresses, but something was preventing them from sharing that information with us. It seemed there was some unwritten code that prevented them from passing on these details to journalists. Perhaps they didn't want to give these men the opportunity of putting their side of things. The woman who, moments before, seemed to have memorised the local telephone directory, began to stutter and stumble, unsure if there was a bloke called 'Jon', or maybe it were 'Jack', who lived somewhere up there, or was it down the other way?

We went to see Mick Carter, who was an NUM official at Cortonwood. Sadly, he died not long after I interviewed him. Mick was a tough, intelligent man – he used his redundancy money from the pit to put himself through university. Like the others, he was happy to speak about everything with regard to the strike except 'scabs'. He told me that one often walked past his house and Mick would shout abuse at him while the man turned his head and pretended not to hear. But when I asked for his name, Mick said he could not stand to even speak it; he said he would take that information to the grave with him. And he was as good as his word.

We eventually got a few names to work on from people who prefer to remain anonymous. Imagine an intensity of feeling that can survive so long that people live in fear of it two decades later. I knocked on lots of doors and was told – mostly in polite tones – to sling my hook. The breakthrough came with Mark Baldwin, the second man to return to work at Cortonwood. He now lived some way from the site of the old pit and had no qualms about discussing why he had done what he did. His reason was simple: money. He struggled with his conscience, as he came from a traditional mining family, but in the end the need to feed his children overrode the pressure to hold the line with his fellow miners. All these years on, he did have some regrets, but he made his decision at the time based on providing for his wife and children. He still gets verbal abuse to this day but he ignores it; his skin is thick after enduring years of hearing 'You bloody scab!' shouted at him on the street.

When he went back to work, the police were having to provide a heavy guard for strike breakers. The men were usually put on a bus with motorcycle outriders and cars, to ensure they got through the crowd of angry pickets.

Mark says he had been reassured there wouldn't be much of a fuss when he went back in. But on the designated day he looked out of his front window to see a fleet of police vehicles with their blue lights flashing, ready to escort him into work. It was like a scene from a TV police drama. He knew he was taking his life in his hands to go against his friends and neighbours, but that was the choice he made at the time. Would he do it again today? Probably – if it was necessary to feed his kids.

I would never get the chance to ask Frank why he did what he did, but I did try to ask his widow. We tracked Winnie down to a neat little house in Wombwell. She wasn't pleased to see me, though. She was visibly distressed at having a stranger come to her door and ask about the family rift. There was no invitation to come in for a warm cup of tea. She was polite, though, and said she didn't want to talk about what happened. The one thing she did say was that what happened in the strike had haunted her husband until the day he died.

When Harry heard about his brother breaking the strike, the first thing he did was to turn him in to the local NUM: any family loyalty was superseded by loyalty to the union and his workmates. His actions were partly to protect his wife and kids by ensuring it was known that it wasn't him who had gone in, but it was also an act of anger that led to reprisals against Frank. Once the word got out, with Harry's help, his walls were daubed with graffiti saying 'scab', and his windows had bricks thrown through them.

I went up to strike centre and I said to them, 'Listen, my name is Nugger, same as me brother, Nugger.' They said, 'What's up?' I says, 'What it is, our Frank's gone in.' And they were stumped. They says, 'No, we can't believe it!' I says, 'It's true. And I'm reporting it in. I'm reporting me own brother. He shouldn't have gone in. I know he ain't got a phone, but I'll try and contact him.'

I didn't want anybody coming down road where I lived and throwing a brick through my window. One of 'em says, 'Harry, don't worry about it. I'll spread it up and down.' I says, 'Right. I'll tell you where he gets dropped off, where he gets picked up, everything.'

And it went a couple of days, and phone rang. It were him, Frank. And I says to him, 'What the hell thou doing going in?' He said he didn't have no money. But his wife were working. He says they ain't got enough to live on and that. I says, 'There's me and Jenny and two bairns and we've no money and we're living alright.' I says, 'Frank, listen, don't go in no more. I'm going to see a union man. You ring me at 6 o'clock tonight and I'll have some more information for thee.' Well, I saw union and they says, 'Can you get him to come out?' I says,

'I'll get him to come out, but he's no money.' They says, 'Just tell him to come back out. We'll see him at your house.'

So I phoned our Frank at 6 o'clock, and I says to him, 'Will you come to our house?' He says 'No, I can't get on that bus now and come to Brampton'. I told him I would catch the bus with him, as nobody would touch him if he were with me.' I went and met him. He came here. I says, 'Right, there's two union men here. They're going to talk to thee and I'm going out.' Now, I know they gave him some money; I don't know how much they gave him though. I went to the bus stop with him. I says 'Thou doesn't go in; thou stops out.' And he didn't go back in.

Frank were getting letters sent through pit. I had a threatening letter from down south somewhere delivered to pit and brought to my house personally, telling me I were this and that and all sorts because I'd got him out. I weren't bothered.

There was tight security around the men who went back, and the pickets didn't always know who was breaking the strike. If a miner suddenly disappeared from the picket lines, rumours would start that he had gone back and reprisals would follow. It was something of a witch-hunt. It seems that no one suspected Frank would be a strike breaker so, even when he went in to work, he was still socialising with men from the picket line in the evening; they had no idea he was a 'scab'. That is, until Harry told them.

When he were going in for them few days or whatever, there were a picket at top of lane, like, because scabs were going in, and I saw one of lads who used to live near Frank. He said to me, he says, 'Hey up, Harry. Have you seen your Frank? I were playing cards with him last night.' I says, 'Thou what? Ah, so thou plays cards in club with a scab?' He says, 'What?' I says, 'He's gone in at pit. He's the one who you've been fighting to try and stop going in this morning.' 'Oh my god,' he says, 'I can't believe it!' I says, 'It's right. Believe me, it's right.'

Well, it spread then, round where he lived. There were scab painted on walls of his house. They barred him out at club. He had his windows put in. He phoned me and told me he'd had his windows put in, like. He says, 'Ah, thou'll know who did it, won't thou?' I says, 'Ah, but it weren't me. It weren't me who put 'em in. I could have come. I know where thou lives,' I says, 'but I never put them in for thee.' I says, 'I'm not doing any more now thou's come out.'

Harry saw his brother once more after the strike. The dispute had been over for six months or so when he, Jenny and their son were in Barnsley, shopping. They bumped into Frank, who was with his wife Winnie. It didn't take long for the sparks to fly. As Jenny and Harry tell the story, Frank was not repentant for what he had done – quite the contrary. He started to have a go at the NUM, criticising union officials – in particular Arthur Scargill. It was a red rag to a Harry bull. To make matters worse, Frank criticised Harry for taking redundancy from the pit.

I just blew me top. Jenny walked away with bairn. His wife walked away. And he pulled whole Union down. Roy Hart, Mick Carter, every union man he could think on, he pulled down. And when he started pulling Arthur Scargill down, that were it. I'd a ding-dong battle with him – no blows, nowt like that, I were just swearing at him and calling him all the names under sun, and Jenny just disappeared. I just couldn't stand it. We'd done twelve month on strike, and then I get him to come back out, union men gives him money so he can manage, and then he pulled 'em down, every union man, even them two who gave him money! I couldn't believe it. I says, 'That's it. Done with you. Finished.' And that were it. You know, if only

I'd have owt in my hand, I should have hit him with it. I just felt like that, you know. Things what I did for him!

Now I did speak to him once again after our Dad died; this were about fourteen years ago. We'd been in Blackpool with two bairns, and when we came back a friend comes up to me and says, 'Some bad news for thee. Your dad passed away a fortnight since.' I says, 'He did? Why didn't somebody let me know?' So I phoned this schoolteacher who lived only two doors off me mam, and she says, 'Where the hell's thou been, Harry? Didn't nobody phone thee?' I says, 'No. Who's looking after me mam?' She says 'Only me.' So I went on Monday, because this schoolteacher said she had been looking after her and had been off school for a fortnight. I said, 'Where was our Frank and our Ted and their wives?' She said they didn't even go to funeral; there were only three from Huddersfield who went. I couldn't believe it.

So me and Jenny had to keep going through to look after me mam, because she were on her own and she were crippled; she were invalid. It were coming up to Christmas, and we fetched her here to our house. She stopped here for about three month, and then I got her to go into a home; she was seventy-eight years old.

Harry wanted to sort out his mother's house, so he called in people who do clearances. They came with a van and took it all away. He says he didn't get any money for his mother's things; he simply wanted it dealt with. But it appears Frank had a different view. Harry says he accused him of selling all the furniture so he could make some money out of the situation. Harry blew his top again.

When he said that, I were on phone here and I lashed into him. I called him all the b's, c's what I could mention, and I slammed the phone down on him. Me mother were in a home for about four year. I think they went once to see her – once! And I says, 'Right, if owt ever happens to me mother,' I says, 'I shan't tell nobody.' When she did finally pass away, I didn't tell nobody. Frank never phoned or owt.

When pressed a bit harder about his relationship with Frank – the eldest of three sons – it was clear that the animosity predated the strike. Harry says that Frank didn't come to his wedding and had always boasted about being better than Harry. There was no love between these brothers. So perhaps it wasn't surprising that Harry felt no great sense of loss. He still felt plenty of emotion in connection with Frank, but it was all anger. Time had done nothing to soften his or Jenny's feelings. As with his father's death, Harry was one of the last to hear that Frank had died in 2002. He spoke of it as if it were of no interest to him whatsoever. Harry heard about it when he was in a supermarket.

I didn't know he'd died. I got to know he'd passed away when I were in Morrison's. Somebody told me. He says, 'Your Frank passed away three weeks since.' I says, 'Ah, ah right-o.' He says, 'Didn't thou know?' I says, 'No. Don't want to know.' He says, 'Oh right.' And that were it.

What struck me most about Jenny and Harry's tough position on Frank was how rigid it was. As you saw, I asked Jenny time and again about forgiveness but she would not even let that thought enter her head. It was quite chilling, especially when I had seen the warmer, softer side of the Evanses. This intransigence highlighted the individual nature of the people in the former coalfields. They had their own culture: you either accepted it or buggered off back to where you came from. There was no middle ground. Jenny saw nothing wrong with her alienation from Frank's family; it was a view that made sense in the context of how she had been brought up. This was how her father and grandfather would have behaved. She was merely continuing the tradition – her words summed it up: 'That is just how it is.'

Having said that, Jenny and women like her learned through the strike that they didn't have to accept 'how it was'. They were forced into change, and ended up embracing it. But it seems there were some aspects of mining life that were unalterable; men and women alike did not and would not budge from their view of 'scabs'.

Jenny didn't rush off to further education or train for a profession after the strike, but in her terms the changes that came were still considerable. She was not driven by ambition; she was a housewife first and foremost, and proud of it. Her life has been dedicated to the home, to bringing up her children and sorting out Harry – I'm sure she would say that was a full-time job in itself. What happened to Jenny was an awakening of the public side of her nature that took her beyond her own four walls; it added to her life, rather than making her unhappy with what she had. She learned she could stand alongside the men and speak to them on their level. She found she was comfortable taking roles that gave her some control. None of this detracted from her home life. The dispute did not make her dissatisfied with her lot; instead it made her realise that she could simply do more, make time for Jenny while not affecting the family.

Before, I was just a housewife who used to clean up. I did my daily chores, looking after husband and children. But when strike happened women got together to do food parcels and soup kitchens. We were going on rallies, backing men up, trying to get money in aid for the miners, in aid of the children – toys and so on. It taught me to stand and say what I believe in. I wouldn't

189

have thought about those things before – like becoming a governor at a primary school. I wouldn't have dreamed I could do that or even thought about taking it on. It taught me all sorts of things. I've stood up for women ever since.

There is still a great sense of loss in the Evans household. Jenny says that although working down a mine wasn't a nice job, it was where you went to earn the money you needed to put food on the table. She said that jobs were hard to find once the pits were closed. Harry had trouble finding work. And having redundancy money actually worked against them.

If you did get any redundancy money, as soon as you went to dole, they said, 'What was your job last time?' and when you said you were a miner, they said go home and spend your redundancy money and then come back.

Although Jenny and Harry still see themselves as a mining family, they acknowledge that their children will forget, and their grandchildren will only know of what happened by learning it from them or in school. They cannot stop the passage of time and the inevitable passing of their way of life; but that doesn't mean they accept the change willingly.

There is still anger. Harry always speaks about what happened down pit, even today. When we go shopping and he sees someone in supermarket who used to work down pit, I can be all way round and done shopping and he'll still be talking to two or three of 'em about pit. They talk about it all the time. Before the strike all of them in this village worked down colliery. Then it came to the strike and everyone in the village backed everyone up – it were like one big family, actually, after the strike. 'Cos of their jobs they've had to move, so now there's only a few miners around. At one time you could sit on the wall and you'd know who's on what shift, so you might think, I won't put my radio on loud because so and so's next door and they're on night shifts. You don't know things like that now; its just not the same.

Harry still holds the view that, in some respects, the miners were actually victorious in the dispute, despite having to return to work and the eventual loss of the pits. He firmly believes the miners gave Margaret Thatcher a bloody nose.

We did everything right. Only things that were done wrong were police force coming in and trying to knock seven bells out of us. But we were as good as them. She might have won battle, Maggie Thatcher. She didn't win war.
Didn't she?
Oh no. Because we beat her, in a way. She didn't like it, us coming out on strike and stopping out that long. Twelve month! She didn't expect that.
But at the end of it, it must have been bitter really to go back?
Oh it were, it were, you know, but what can you do? We had to go back; we had to go back. They voted, Arthur Scargill's committee and that.
Nobody liked it that day. We all went to top of village, miner's centre, and we all walked down, you know. But we held our heads up high, us. Ours didn't drop down – not like Maggie Thatcher when she were voted out of government.

As the women's perception of their role was altered by the strike, the men also began to see them differently. Before 1984 most men would not have agreed to allow women on the picket line; it would have been considered not their place. Even when the strike began, there was resistance to women doing more. But they proved to be an unstoppable force; there was nothing the miners could do to keep their wives indoors. As it turned out, those who were against women standing alongside the men had to eat humble pie. Even the toughest men had to admit that the women were crucial in keeping the strike going as long as it did. It turned out that the men were surprised by the hidden talents of their women. And many are magnanimous enough to pay tribute to the contribution they made.

If it wasn't for the women, the strike wouldn't have lasted. It were them, them women, who gave 110 per cent then. I know we gave 100 per cent, but them women gave 110, and they were great. Because you could go up to strike centre, get a meal, you know, and everybody pulled together. There were no bitterness or owt like that. It were all pull together, and that's what got us through twelve month. They were great, them women.

CHAPTER SEVEN

Pride and Prejudice:
'Mary'

Originally, all the women in this book were happy to be identified. They wanted to share their stories as proof of what they could do, to reveal where they had come from and how far they had travelled, no matter how difficult the journey had been. They recognised it was important to lay down a marker in history to highlight the women's role in the mining communities. They were proud to put their names to their achievements.

But one woman – let's call her Mary – was different. She volunteered to take part in the book but in the end, for reasons that will become apparent, backed away from owning her story. I felt her personal history was significant and needed to be told, even if it meant removing any details that would identify her. Anonymity was better than silence. Mary represented a large section of the female population in the former mining areas. She was one of those who, during the strike, had been given a flavour of a world where they were free to speak their minds and feel their power, but had subsequently let that independence slip away from their grasp. They were drowning in a dying culture.

Before I met Mary I had been told that she was known by some as 'the Madonna'. Not in any way a prima donna, but a Ma-donna, with the emphasis on 'Ma'. The distinction was important. There was nothing of the diva about her; she was as down-to-earth as the pits she had fought so hard to defend over the years. But Mary was reputed to be as near perfect a wife and mother as you could get. There were those who marvelled at how spotless her house was and her children had always been immaculate. As I got to know her I realised that they had a point. When I mustered enough nerve to tell Mary about the soubriquet she laughed and shook her head – she didn't see things like that. From her viewpoint, her life was a long way off being a tidy squeaky-clean affair, although she had done her best with the cards she had been dealt. The religious nature of the term was relevant. Not only because her Catholic family background had done much to mould her, but, if it was true that cleanliness was next to godliness, Mary already had one foot firmly through the pearly gates.

I also knew that Mary didn't suffer fools gladly. Her 'no messing' approach came across loud and clear when I phoned to arrange our meeting. I was keen that it should be on a Monday, but she wanted a rest as she would be recovering from a busy family gathering over the previous weekend. Anxious not to miss the chance of meeting her, but pressed by a tight schedule, I pushed it and eventually she agreed. I apologised for twisting her arm. The reply to this was, 'Look love, you wouldn't be able to twist my arm unless I was prepared to let you, so don't you worry about that.' Enough said.

The family home was in a small Yorkshire village where the unfriendly industrial landscape gives way to softer, greener scenery. There are gentle hills and wide open spaces. Rich natural resources made this area the site of numerous collieries in the heyday of King Coal; they had all disappeared now though. Mary's house was part of a contemporary terrace and, as expected, her home was pristine – although not an icon in sight.

Mary was a statuesque woman – 5ft 6 plus a few inches for her mass of auburn wavy hair. She wore little make-up – only a trace of lipstick – and was modestly dressed; nothing remarkable, nothing out of the ordinary. It was the way she held herself that set her apart. Her regal manner was more in step with a stately home than the terraced house that constituted her domain.

When I arrived on a grey October morning, her husband was there but only briefly. He was pleasant but seemed uncomfortable – I wasn't sure whether that was because I was a journalist or because he was used to leaving his wife to deal with these matters. I did find that it was often the former miners who had trouble with strangers, whereas the women were more inclined to give people the benefit of the doubt. They judged outsiders as they found them, and not by the job they did, nor by the betrayals of others.

We sat in the front room, by a reassuring coal fire. I hadn't expected Mary to be emotional, but before we even began talking about her life, I noticed her eyes were watery and she appeared anxious. With hindsight, I realised that this encounter was different to anything she had done before. She knew I wanted to hear about the 'life and times of Mary': wife, mother and unlikely but seasoned activist. This was not simply about her role in the strike of 1984/5. It was a brief that she had clearly been mulling over; she was prepared to talk to me about intimate details from her background. Mary was an honest woman – other than when she was driven to stealing vegetables from fields for her children in times of poverty.

As she sat down and we warmed up, both physically and mentally, she gave me a defensive smile and crossed her arms. She might be tough, but much of what she had to say was laced with ironic humour; some of it to cover the pain, some genuine amusement, viewing events as she was from a distance. She wanted to make it clear to me that her life was complex. 'It's very difficult to lay things out clearly when so much of my life is kept in different boxes in my head. When you open one up you then have to open others.' She rolled her eyes and laughed at herself. Her ability at self-mockery was disarming and charming at the same time.

No one's life is straightforward – it strikes me it was never intended that things would follow a straight, flat route. All the same, it is hard to imagine by appearances alone what individuals have gone through. To look at Mary, all prim and proper, you could no more imagine her using swear words in a fury, nose-to-nose with policemen during a demo, than you would expect the Pope to give his blessing to the contraceptive pill. And yet she could belt it out with the best of them. The strike had peeled back the thick skin of a rigid Catholic upbringing and exposed a raw energy, powerful enough to light the way for others.

Unlike the vast majority of the wives I had come into contact with, Mary had no knowledge of the pits prior to her marriage.

I didn't know anything about the pit. No one in my family had worked in the mines; my father was a lorry driver. So I came to it without knowing what it was all about. Over the years, of course, I have learned the hard way. We got married when I was nearly twenty-one. He had thirteen jobs the first two years we were married, he did all sorts of things. But then he went down the pit. He worked at a number of pits, which have all disappeared now of course. Later he came out of the pit and went into sales, and then he worked as an electrician underground, and the last few years working there he was at pit top.

For Mary, marriage was an important escape from a homelife that had been overshadowed with violence, but it was a case of 'frying pans and fires'. She had a dream of creating the loving

196

family of which she had been deprived as a child; but as with most fairy tales, the reality had less of the Cinderella about it and more of the Big Bad Wolf. What she did find was something unexpected; through adversity she discovered facets of her character that she never thought existed. Inside she found a dogged determination, the ability to stand up and be counted; she would speak and people would listen. Quite a shock for a woman who was once so shy that if she was in a pub, she would have to get her husband to ask where the ladies' toilet was. To understand Mary and how she came to be so outspoken and formidable, yet funny and warm, it was important to turn back the clock to her childhood. To a place and time filled with pain, both physical and mental – much of it attributable to her mother.

My mother was a violent woman. She would often give me a good hiding. It was much more common in those days. Now I admit that I have smacked our three lads – some days they didn't know they were up unless they'd had a smack. But it was different with my mother. She would hit you with anything that was handy; it could be anything, like the dog lead, the carpet-beater, or I have known her raise a milk bottle to my brothers. We had a pianola which was her pride and joy – the ones you put the rolls of music in. Well, those rolls of music were really heavy, and she did attack my brother with one of those once. With her it was never a slap. I know you can't slap kids any more, but I do know it can be hard with three kids – my dad was a long-distance lorry driver, so she had to be mother and father with three children in the war years, with rationing. I have come to terms with all that.

I have smacked ours but I have never hit them with my fist, as she would hit us, and I do think there is a big difference. A clip or slap always on the backside, yeah – I mean, my kids laugh about it now. They said how you could get upstairs with your feet six steps in front of your head and keep your balance; but they said, 'If you were chasing us, mam, we could always do that because, you tuck in the bottom so's you don't get a whack.' Bless 'em.

I asked if Mary thought her mother had been beaten as a child, and that was why she passed this on to her.

I do wonder if my mother was like that because she had been beaten. My grandmother was Irish; she had met and married in Ireland and came to Yorkshire for her honeymoon and he never took her back. And she had six children and he died. Then she married my grandfather and had two children to him – a boy and girl, my mother. She was the youngest. Just little things she said made me feel that all her life she wanted to be in her mother's good books. She always wanted to be the favourite. In all her life she never ever said one wrong word about her mother. Never. I would imagine that she had had beatings and that was what she passed on to us, but she never said anything about that. She cried for her mother up to the day she died. There was always tears. I hate New Year because her mother died at New Year. She died when people were passing, singing 'Auld Lang Syne', and we were brought up to think that New Year was the worst time you can imagine. I haven't passed that one to mine – you learn there are loads of things you hang onto yourself and don't pass on.

I was scared of my mum, really scared. You could be skipping along, I would see my brother and he would say, 'Mam wants to see you,' and oh, my every bit of happiness would just drain out of me. I would get to the back door of the house and be full of dread; then he would say, 'Only kidding!' I'd be angry but relieved. It was a genuine deep-seated fear of her. Because my hair was long and thick, she would grab it and bang my head against the wall.

198

It still bothers me today, despite the fact that my mother is dead. My daughter-in-law was telling me recently about her grandma who was ninety-two and was a contemporary of my mother's. Apparently she said, 'I can remember Mary when she was a girl – ooh she had lovely hair but oh, her mother did used to hit her!' Now what does that say about her? I found it sad that all these years on and that was how this woman remembered me.

My mother had the ability to strip me of any pleasure. Silly things. Well, then again, they were not silly, I am trying to make light of it. My mother didn't speak to me for nineteen years. Pride made me strong because I thought I had escaped by marrying, got away from this dominant woman – I hated never knowing what you were going to find when you went in. With my father, he didn't get involved; it was anything for a quiet life. I looked forward to normal things like just being able to have your dinner at two o'clock, instead of one.

When Mary was at school she was singled out as a bright spark. Her headmaster put her in for entrance exams to the local college and a Catholic grammar school but it all went horribly wrong. The memory of missed opportunities all those years ago still had enormous power over Mary; she cried as she told me how her mother had effectively consigned her to a life without the education she hungered for.

I left school at fifteen – didn't go on to further education; this was something that my mother stripped me of. I have no qualifications, nothing, but I could have if it wasn't for my mother. It was only a few years ago, not long before she died, she was criticising my brother and saying that he had stopped his son from going to university, and said he should have encouraged him. I was amazed she could say that after what she had done to me.

I said to my mother, 'Things don't always work out like that, Mum, do they? You have to remember – you have to think back.' You see, I went to Catholic school, and you didn't automatically sit your 11-plus. I was fortunate to be one of two chosen to sit the entrance exam. There were only a few free places. Most of them were paid.

My mother told the whole of village that I had been chosen to sit, and how it was such an honour, de da de da. So you can imagine what happened when I didn't get a place. My life was hell – I don't think she ever forgave me. So at eleven I was a failure, with her at least. Then the headmaster at my school stopped me one day coming out of dinner, and he said 'Mary, how do you fancy sitting for Technical College? I can get you a paper.' He was just passing when he said this. I was so pleased. I came home and told my mum. But that was all I heard about it, so I didn't think it was going to happen. Then months and months later, the headmaster was on dinner duty. As I passed him to come out, he said 'Mary, will you go to the science room, and I will be with you in ten minutes.' I thought, What have I done? He said, 'Right, go to the toilet first, because you are going to sit for the tech.' That was it. No warning. I went to the toilet. He then closed the classroom door and he said, 'When I say start, you start, and take no notice of anything around you.'

And I passed. They read my name out at school. I was thrilled to bits and I went home and told my mother, but she wasn't pleased as I had hoped; in fact she said she wouldn't let me go because it wasn't a Catholic school, and she insisted that I had a Catholic education. I was devastated. All those years later when she was criticising my brother, I was thinking, 'How can you criticise him when you didn't let me go?' I was shaky and upset, and I said to her, 'Don't you remember when you wouldn't let me go to tech because it wasn't Catholic?' My mother looked me in the eye for an age and said, 'You dreamed that.' And she never blinked; it was a direct gaze. I came home and I cried like a baby. This was only about six years ago. It still affects me now to talk about it.

Mary's dream of an education evaporated the day her mother refused to let her move on to technical college, but the roller-coaster of life did not stand still. Another opportunity quickly presented itself when she was still just fourteen years old.

I didn't really know what I was going to do. Then the people where my mum had her hair done asked if I wanted to work there; I was fourteen at the time, and still at school, and would I go in on a Saturday and help out. It was the hardest thing I have ever done in my life, because I had always been kept in a corner. We were never encouraged to perform, none of us kids in the family had any confidence. And then to work in a hairdresser's surrounded by mirrors was torture. Everywhere you looked, someone was looking at you; everything you did was seen. It was a performance to do someone's hair. Everyone watches. People sat under driers would watch. But I got over that and served my apprenticeship. I was eighteen when the woman I worked for married a bloke that worked for a bank, and he joined the overseas branch and they had a posting so she wanted to sell the shop. I had always got on with her parents and they said I could pay for it as I worked. That was how I came to be a businesswoman, it just happened. I didn't have to buy the shop; they were kind and allowed me to pay the rent and so much off as I went. It fell into my lap. My mother was very proud of that alright – all of a sudden we were businesspeople.

But the truce wasn't to last. Mary longed for a new life. Having financial independence put her in a strong position to free herself from her mother.

So I escaped that life – I was madly, deeply in love with my boyfriend, crazy about him. We had a brilliant two years' courtship. Stomach churned every time I saw him. It was wonderful. We got married; eleven months later, a baby – a year and three weeks later, another baby. It wasn't that we were going to have a baby a year. When I went to see the doctor and I said I had missed a period, he said, 'Are you using French letters?' And I told him that no, I wasn't, and that I was a Catholic. Well, that lasted two babies and after that I thought to hell with it, I couldn't cope. It was a case of 'French letters, hello'. This was before pill.

My mother cast me off when I got married. We had the wedding and not long after we were moving some things from the house one weekend. She decided that you couldn't do that because it was a Sunday. Now that hadn't stopped her let people do decorating for her in the past, but there you go. We had dared to go against her, and that was it. She came to hit me again, and being married I felt I could stand up to her, so I said, 'No, you mustn't hit me!' She never did hurt me physically again, although she was cruel to me mentally.

We moved into the house attached to the shop and put brown paper up at the windows and slept on the floor. I had to leave the area though, because my mother wouldn't leave me alone. She started coming into the shop and saying, 'I'm terribly sorry to intrude, may I have the gold watch that I bought you for your eighteenth birthday, because while you lived with me you got me into debt.' Can you imagine? This was my business, and it was always on a Friday when I was at my busiest. We were packed; everyone would look at me and I wanted to cry.

I saw her over the years; I would bump into her. I always knew when she was nearby. I would say to myself, 'My mother's around this corner.' I had a sixth sense. I think it was fear, I was scared of her. I would walk up to her and say hello and she would look at me and say, 'Hello. You have the better of me – you appear to know me but I do not know you.' I would let the children go to my mother's, but she would not recognise me. I didn't think it was right to keep my kids away.

I would rather have had the beating than the mental abuse. Even to talk about her, I am deeply hurt and I feel I shouldn't be saying these things even though she is now dead. We weren't close, and then I came into this relationship and I didn't want to be a hairdresser or anything. I wanted to be a mum, I wanted to look after my husband, to look after my children. I wanted us to be happy families.

Mary gave up the shop and concentrated on being the perfect wife and mum. But the loss of her financial independence hit harder than she could have imagined. The new responsibilities of supporting a wife, and the arrival of two children in quick succession, took its toll on her husband.

I don't think he could cope and he went off the rails. I never thought of leaving him; I was still crazy about him. But he took to gambling and that was terribly hard. Only those who have been there will know what it's like.

They had been together for more than forty years, despite the ups and downs. Mary said she still loved the man she married. She said when their children were very young, his gambling had forced them onto the breadline. He was working, holding down jobs, but the money was going to the bookies and not towards the household bills. There were times when things looked hopeless, and yet something kept her going. She found strength in her role as a mother; she concentrated on feeding her children and keeping the family together. She found it hard to speak in detail about the gambling as she didn't want to be disloyal to her husband. The box that contained the darker secrets of this painful period in her life remained closed. I knew the key to her survival was the inner strength that had got Mary through so much in her life. It was a gift that she didn't recognise she had until the strike.

The worst time was before the two miners' strikes in the early seventies. Mary faced great financial hardship as the debts began to mount up. Things became so bad that Mary would have to take the children 'for a walk' to avoid the debt collectors who were knocking at her door. Pride was something that threaded its way through the tapestry of Mary's life. She asked me at one point if I thought 'pride' was a sin. Like her, I was brought up as a Catholic, so I understood her preoccupation with sin. I thought for a while and told her I didn't think so – especially as in her case it was the very thing that helped her survive in the face of crushing odds. The way she fought back against her mother was to be proud – that meant always to look well groomed, for her boys to look clean; head held high and never look at the ground, but straight ahead. Even when she was hiding stolen vegetables under her coat in order to give the kids something for their supper, Mary did it with her nose in the air.

I wasn't ever going to look down. I never walked over my step without I had a bath, whether I had soap or not. My hair was always clean and I always wore lipstick. One would last me twelve months because I had to get the last bit out with a matchstick. And I always walked with my head up, and the kids used to shine and everybody believed that I thought I was it. I was that lady with the handbag and the lipstick and not a penny in her purse. I would walk up the road with these beautiful, glowing, clean children. We must have looked as though we were going somewhere nice, but actually I was taking them off across the fields while the debt man came, it was as simple as that, to avoid him.

It got to the stage that I had all sorts of people knocking at my door: the police, county court judgements, and I knew that I had to work to feed children. This was before the strikes in the seventies. We had a lovely new two bedroom bungalow. The deposit came from selling the hairdressing business. When we got it I was so happy but as things got worse financially, I knew we might not be there long. I became obsessed with cleaning. I laugh about it now, but really and truly it wasn't funny. I think the worry was so bad that if I didn't clean I would have had a nervous breakdown. I used to rip my hands when I took down the guttering and drainpipes. I would lay them on the lawn and scrub them with Brillo until they were shining, then I would put them back up. Even today I don't cope very well with worry. I have had too much happen to me before. When there is a worry in the family I have trouble keeping myself under control. I get panic attacks and I still go back to cleaning. I am not as bad now, such as I don't hoover in the loft or take the toilet cistern to pieces. I did, you know. I used to take the flush thing out, unscrew the whole thing, polish each part and put it back together. Then I would drain the water out and scrub the cistern. You could have had your dinner in there, it was so clean.

I am not compulsive any longer. Now I like the house to be comfortable, but to be warm and welcoming and when the boys and their families come, so long as the grandchildren aren't destructive, it doesn't matter too much.

Mary had been proud to become a businesswoman. Listening to her, I could see that, given a different set of circumstances, she would have gone on to further education and put her brain-power into a career. But life had different plans. She knew how to cut and style hair but, once the business was sold and she had young children, she was trapped in the house. It may have been spotless but it was a prison. She couldn't afford childcare, and her mother was not going to change enough to offer to help her, so doing a full-time job was out of the question. By the time the miners, including her husband, went out on strike in 1972, things at home were already dire for the young family. There was a point where Mary feared she might end up in a hostel with her children. To have gone from having nothing to being a businesswoman of some means, and then back to having nothing again, would have destroyed most people – but not Mary.

We lost the bungalow when I was pregnant. It gradually got worse and worse. I knew I was going to lose my home, because the debts were growing and the mortgage payments weren't being made. To be big with him, and in that position, was so hard. We had to move to a colliery house. I'm not saying anything against those kind of houses; it was up to the people who lived in them to make them nice. But this one was filthy. Remember, I had been living in a brand new bungalow. The neighbours where we lived were awful. You see, I was seen as being posh and stuck-up. I would always be cleaning and cleaning. But I would have the kids peeing on the step and shovelling stuff through the letter-box. I had my son in the winter of 1972. When I was big with him I would have to walk in fields digging up potatoes. I would hide them under my coat. The funny thing was, I didn't see it as stealing; it was more about surviving.

You see, I had nothing to feed the kids, absolutely nothing. Nothing to eat and pregnant. My husband came home every day, and I always thought I had to feed him too. Looking back, I would alter that. I fed him and didn't feed myself. I lived on new bread and lard when I was big with child. Can you imagine? When I was taking potatoes from the fields I would still walk tall. I would sail around like the queen mother. We weren't allowed to stoop – that was one good thing from my mum. Book on the head, walk your height. I am only 5ft 6½ins, but everyone thinks I am taller because of my hair.

I couldn't imagine what it would be like to be so desperate as to have to steal in order to feed my children. Mary had gone through true poverty, hiding the reality behind a thin guise of having enough to get by. And yet she could now laugh about her plight as a heavily pregnant mother of two with not a scrap of food in the cupboard.

Needless to say, on a diet like that I was very thin and suffered from terrible heartburn. People would tease me and say that it was going to be a really hairy baby – if you have heartburn the tale is that the baby is going to have lots of hair. No one knew that I was having to eat new bread and lard. When he came out he was covered in what looked like lard. There was loads of it, all jagged around his eyes. The midwife said, 'Look at your baby! What on earth have you been eating?' I didn't dare tell her. They couldn't get hold of the cord because every time they went to get hold of it, it slipped away. They were laughing. I wonder what they would have thought if they knew I had been near starving during the pregnancy. He was gorgeous when they managed to wash the stuff off. Nurses from other wards came to look at him. It was just as though he had been preserved in this fat. He hadn't a wrinkle or anything.

Her mother had always drummed into her head that she mustn't 'lower' herself to work in a factory. So she found it hard when it came to the crunch and the only job that she could do was in a large bakery. Mary had to swallow her pride – she had no choice.

I knew I had to get a job to feed kids, so I went to the bakery. I worked twenty hours a day, in the evenings, so I could sort the kids out and go to work when my husband got in. I worked on the production line, I had to wear a nasty green smock with a hairnet. I wouldn't have minded so much if I was allowed to wear one of the yellow smocks; they were much nicer. When I was there three months I saw a couple of men who were fitters from the pit. I knew them from being in business. It hurt when they came up to me and said, 'What the hell are you doing working here?' They were surprised to see me like that. I said it just fits in with the children, so that wasn't a lie.

The important thing was that I didn't have to rely on anyone else; I had money of my own and that meant I could feed the kids and pay bills. I had a lot to swallow to go and work in a factory. It sounds awful, and I wouldn't feel that way now because I met some wonderful women. But at the time I had been running my own business, and I had this big pride thing, and all of a sudden I was going to become something that my mother said I should never be – a factory worker. Again, I was a failure to her. And yet that was what I had to do. And then I felt I was letting her down as well; I had all that to deal with. That guilt trip even though she wasn't talking to me.

I worked evenings from five-thirty until half-past nine. So I could get the kids home from school. They were fed, everything was ready as they came in. I took their hats and coats off, they washed up, and as they did that their dinner was on the table. Then my husband would be home; as they came in I flew out. I got the bus and then got home for about ten o'clock during a night. It was great during the strike because at least I was bringing in some money. I was doing quality control, which I enjoyed because it was using my head. It was paperwork, and I liked it. And it meant I had the run of the factory.

By the time Mary faced the strike of 1984/5, she was so familiar with having no money that being on the breadline was nothing new. By unwelcome chance, she had served an apprenticeship in poverty that was to stand her in good stead. Unlike many women who had been accustomed to having food to put on the table, Mary knew how to make do with the bare minimum. So when the strike came she found she was in a good position to advise others on how to cope. Her job in the bakery kept her family fed and clothed. By then her two eldest sons had joined their father in the collieries, so she had three men on strike – joining picket lines every day. Although her pride had been badly bruised by having to take a factory job, the work freed her; it put her in control again, as she was earning her own money. It also gave her back some independence. Still she hadn't explored her capabilities, until the 1984/5 strike began. It was only then that something happened; something inside her changed forever.

I would never ever be downtrodden again, so the strike was a doddle for me. I felt guilty when I used to see the other women. A lot of them say they thought I was very strong and I could help them. And I was strong, because we had been so poor before strike, I had learned that you could live on potatoes. And to stop kids worrying, you could all get huddled in a bunch and tell them that you were pretending to be camping when you didn't have a fire. They didn't need to know that you had no money for coal. I had done all of it so many times before the strike.

As she spoke, it struck me how hard it must have been to work during the strike in a place packed with food, like being Alice in a sugary wonderland, where technically you were not allowed to drink or eat any of it. And you had to deal with the stark contrast that, outside the factory perimeter, families starved for want of a loaf of bread. The thought of mountains of brightly coloured cakes brings out the child in us all. What must it have been like working in this land of candy-coloured plenty for a few hours a day, then going home to the greyness of need? It seemed stupid to ask if she pinched the odd cake or two, but I couldn't resist the question.

Oh God, yes! I was very thin when the strike started. I had a hysterectomy a few months before and I hadn't been well. So I had only been back at work for three weeks or so when the men walked out. We were three or four months into the strike when the supervisor tapped me on the shoulder. He was a lovely, kind man. He asked me, 'Are you on strike?' When I told him I was, he said 'Well you eat as many cakes as you want.'

The bakers' union asked for a concession of cakes for the miners' kitchens and, although it was a conservative company, the union fought successfully for this. Normally, if there was anything wrong with the cakes – you know, they weren't the right weight or not the right shape or they had the wrong fillings, nothing actually wrong with the cake itself – they would be sent to another company, who sold them on, in markets and the like. But during strike they would go to the NUM. I used to say, 'These don't look that good.' And my supervisor, whose husband was also on strike, used to agree. As I say, the cakes themselves were fine – it was just something wrong with how they looked, usually. So they had to be put into cardboard boxes with NUM written on the side. I would ring my husband to come with a van. My supervisor and me would put them in boxes – we would take them up in the lift. We'd be hysterical with laughter, chugging along through all these doors with a trolley full of cakes. Security would check the boxes all marked up for NUM, and then we would take them home. There were so many you couldn't move in our hall. We would take them along to the various kitchens. There's that saying, 'Let them eat cake!' Well, they certainly did.

The strike was a defining time for Mary. The violence and poverty she had been through in her life had groomed her for the fray. And it was in that twelve months she rediscovered the ambition lost through her mother's actions. Her latent intelligence and dynamism found a home.

I came into my own in the strike. I don't know if I was hit by lightning, or whether I had just seen enough of the scrubbing brush; I don't know, but something happened. It might have been a miracle, I have no idea. My next-door neighbours were on strike. We had seen it on TV and our husbands came back and talked about the strike. We both – the women – read an article about a women's group being set up. I had gone to hang out the clothes and over the fence we were saying it looks like a strike, and my husband says it could be quite a long one. By this time I had paid off the county court judgements, and I had money in the bank; not a lot, but I had some, and I didn't owe anyone anything

They thought it could be eight-week strike or plus. Reading about the women made me want to do something and my neighbour agreed. I mentioned it to my husband and he said he would mention it at the NUM union meeting. So he did, and he said why not come down and see what goes on. Well I did. I had never been so scared in all my life. I had never been in a meeting, never seen any of this 'speaking through the chair'. There were all these men. My friend who came with me was more confident than I was. I was sitting there shaking. I said right from the start that we wanted to work with the union and not for the union. I had that feeling straight away and that was it, off and running. I wrote a poster and put it up around the village. We didn't know what path we were going to follow, only that we were wanting to be active and to be seen to be doing something.

I put the poster out – that was my job – and the union said we could use their room in the working men's club upstairs. We put on the posters that the meeting was going to be there. We went down and sat there and just hoped that someone would come. The thing I remember the most clearly was the sound of the women walking up the wooden stairs to the room where we were. I thought, 'Oh my, they are coming!' That first night there were about ten, then the week after, seventeen, then the next week, twenty-two.

It was the second meeting that Mary had ever attended – this one actually organised by herself and her friend. As the women came into the room, she didn't know any of them and the terror of what she had done made her shake again, but something drove her on and made her push the fear to one side.

The first thing we did was to help the pickets by raising funds and provide a packed lunch to take, because the men were away hours and hours. My husband went every day. The lads went picketing and my youngest went to school while I went to the kitchen. We were only two or three weeks doing sandwiches when we decided we needed to do more than that. We needed a kitchen to give people hot food.

As time went on, things were getting harder for people. It was a meeting place, which is important. You look around and there are two hundred people all sat there having a meal and in the same boat as you.

The people who missed out on that were the losers. We tried to persuade people to come to the kitchen – okay, so the meal might not have been brilliant, but it was warm and provided a place to talk.

On a personal level, I felt a great sense of achievement, because I had escaped from the little house where I scrubbed and didn't have any money. And I could say to women, have you tried this or that, and you can make this or that.

The miners had food being donated by numerous sympathetic groups all over the world, from Russia to Chile. The kindness was appreciated but the benefit was not always felt. The goods that came in tins were often unidentifiable, because no one could translate what was written on them. In one kitchen, the story goes that the women had fried some food in what they believed was cooking oil from France. When the meal turned out to be inedible, a French dictionary revealed why – the tin had contained floor polish.

On kitchen day we used to have a raffle for a food parcel. It got towards the end of the strike the tins must have been red hot, because they were foreign so no one knew what the hell was in them. So they always donated the parcel back for the next raffle. It could have been anything, we never found out. We did the kitchen five days a week, 9 a.m. to 3.30 p.m. I used to come home. I had to have a strip-wash with a kettle of boiling water, because we didn't have the coal to heat the water, and then it was off to work at five. I didn't get home till ten, and at ten o'clock the local fish and chip shop used to give us potatoes. They used to rumble them, but they had eyes in them, and in the winter I would sit here with a big blanket around me and some hot water and this dustbin full of potatoes. In freezing cold water, and I used to have to sit and take all of the eyes out of the potatoes.

My husband would be up five o'clock for picketing. We would wrestle this dustbin outside to drain it. They would sometimes have to put it on the wheelbarrow and wheel it across the field and leave it at kitchen door and pray that no one would steal it before everyone got there of a morning. The day started early and ended quite late.

It was during the strike that Mary's mother reappeared in her life, adding to her already hefty workload. It was not to do with a change in her mother's behaviour; nor did she show any remorse. Mary was fulfilling the role of a dutiful daughter.

My dad died during the strike. Before that, I went to see him after he had the stroke. My husband came with me; he isn't very good at facing things but he did not let me go on my own and it was a really big thing for me that he was there by my side. After that, I started going to my mum's again, and I was automatically doing her work. I thought she had loads of friends but everyone bailed out – they disappeared, so there was just my mother and me.

It wasn't a making up, it was just as though the years of not talking had never happened; it was never spoken about. I had arrived home and that was it and the next thing, I was cleaning bedrooms and bringing washing home from hers during the strike. So I really had my work cut out.

When the strike was over, the kitchens finished. But I had no intentions of finishing, because there were all the sacked miners to cater for. There was a campaign for those who had been arrested. My husband and sons picketed every day and it could have been one of them, so I always felt that there was a debt to pay. There was also a debt to the villagers, who had been brilliant. They just gave and gave. After the strike we always did a tea for pensioners at Christmas and we have done things at the local school.

The strike may have been lost but that became a secondary issue for Mary and her contemporaries. With the end of the action and the bedraggled return to work, there was a new mood in the mining communities. I remember how people felt a great sense of loss and disgust, but there was also that terrible gnawing ache caused by defeat. The men did try to hold their heads high when they marched defiantly back to work after the strike, but you could see they walked with hollow legs. When they talk about it now, many wish they hadn't made a fuss about going back; they felt stupid carrying banners and chanting that they would never be defeated. The women, though, didn't feel this – well, some of them didn't. Mary says they had no intention of letting Margaret Thatcher steal yet more from them. She had unwittingly given the women a new freedom; she had been a catalyst in their liberation from the kitchen. It couldn't have been a side effect that she could have foreseen or nurtured. Freeing these working-class women from the shackles of domesticity was no part of Thatcherism; it was merely a side effect that went with the bitter pill.

Mary had tasted life on the outside – away from the spectre of a domineering mother, from a self-imposed gruelling regime of work and domestic obsession. There was nothing that was going to make her relinquish this new-found life. She had waited too long to feel her wings; they were not going to be clipped now. It required a slight change of emphasis, but the need for a campaigning group remained.

I always say that I found myself again. I say to young women when I see the kids dragging on them, 'Remember first and foremost you are who you are; after that you are a mum, wife, nurse, cleaner. But first and foremost you are yourself. You will not be thought of any better if you have got one swinging off your elbow and another moaning and groaning. You must think of yourself.' I did become more articulate; instead of being the one that never voiced an opinion, I was the one who had something to say and wasn't afraid to say it.

On the rare occasions that we went out, over the years my husband was very happy for me to sit in the corner somewhere. If we went for a drink and I wanted to go to the toilet, he used to say he would find out where they were. If we were in a working men's club and there was entertainment, I couldn't walk to the toilet unless the lights were down and I could get to the toilet and back before the lights went up. I didn't have the confidence to walk through a room full of people where they could see me. I didn't want to be looked at and I didn't really like men. I didn't like the flattery; they were so two-faced. They were all married but if you walked past them on your own, there was always something they said, some little aside about how I looked. There was a quip or a whistle; I could never cope with that. I was always very honest and would tell them to shut up or say it to their wives. I really have this kind of character, where people would say you can't even talk to her because she thinks she is all that. But I didn't, they were wrong about me.

I have found a voice. After the strike I could stand up to my husband. I did become much more aggressive for a while, but I have calmed down a bit now, mellowed. I don't think you should try and live in someone else's head; perhaps now I understand there is a great difference between men and women, and I couldn't expect my husband to think like me because he is not me, but I always thought he should have been. That he should have wanted to be happy to be sat on the moors with the kids running around, throwing pebbles around, sandwiches and a flask, and everyone rosy and windswept and slightly grubby and happy, which I think is brilliant; but ok if he didn't like it, he didn't. I really thought he should have done; he should have got as much out of it as I did. He liked to go out without the kids.

You do realise the difference between loving and liking. It is important to know that you can love someone and at the same time dislike them. It has nothing at all to do with love and there is no guilt attached to not liking your own child, and maybe finally there is no guilt attached to not liking your own mother.

I have said to the lads many times, 'You will have awful memories of me because I am a human being but I hope the good memories will just about tip the scale the other way.' I am awful for a bargain – I mean it: I never pay full price for anything, doesn't matter what it is, anything, from a pair of sheets to a diamond ring. I will not pay the full price because I think the prices are extortionate, and because of where I came from.

I said to 'em, when I have kicked me clogs and everyone gathers, you will be looking at the coffin, and say to yourselves, 'Ooh, we always wanted to get washed with soap that didn't have tuppence off, and now we can.'

Death came up a few times as we talked. All the women in her circle have had health scares; two have died. Not only do times change, but preoccupations change as well. Once, fighting to feed her children was the big issue; now it was doing what she could in the time she had left. And still her humour came through as she painted the picture of a beleaguered old people's home struggling to cope with this gang of rebellious, hard-bitten, grumpy old women who had minds of their own.

We always envisage the time when we will end up in an old folks home together. God help the people running it! It is one of our pet things; we imagine we will all be sat there with us legs open showing us drawers – because old women do that, don't they – they always sit up and you can see what they had for their breakfast.

We will be sat without us teeth and be saying, 'Look at her, she has had biggest slice of cake, but she were always like that during strike.' That's what we will be saying. Lord Mayor will be coming and opening a new wing or something, and they'll be saying, 'Look at her pushing in, it was always same when a reporter came, it were always her that give interviews.' So I think we might end up like that.

As she spoke of her closeness to women, I wondered what Mary made of Margaret Thatcher – same sex but different side of the fence. How bizarre that Thatcher was the unwitting architect of a sisterhood that had survived longer than she had – in terms of being active. In the mining communities, memories are long; time does not seem to blunt their loves and hates; if anything, it gives them a sharper edge. Forgiveness is unheard of for certain crimes. Being a scab is top of the list but being a 'rogue woman' Prime Minister wasn't far behind. It was with real passion and aggression that Mary talked about Lady Thatcher.

Thatcher did have her day, but we will have ours. We are definitely planning to have a wake, and that will be a hell of a big party. I was really upset, because she was a woman. It was the thing that bothered me most of all, that a woman could do this to other women. 'Maggie' in our area was margarine. It was a cheap substitute for butter. I always said Maggie Thatcher was a substitute for a woman. And we had more than enough of both of them.

Even when she was kicked out, I was sad in a sense, as it proved to me she was a puffed-up nobody. Her whole life revolved around this great big power thing, ego trip. Then again, I hated it when people said we were following Arthur Scargill, because I didn't. I had always said that I was supporting the strike, not him; it was something I believed in. I didn't want nuclear energy. We have got our own fuel in this country. We are one of the few people around here who still have a coalfire. It's not just a financial thing, for me it is something more. I love the real fire. It is like toast in this place, and you get all the water for nothing as there's a back boiler.

Mary's loyalties lie with her female friends. Through them she managed to build the family for which she had always

218

hungered. The strike was a catalyst; the death of one way of life led to the birth of another.

I felt more for women during the strike. I have always been a woman's woman. When I was at the bakery I could be on the shop floor and would watch the women clocking on. I would know by their body language why they were there. I would see one skipping down the two flights of stairs and I knew that she was there to pay for doubleglazing or a fortnight's holiday in Barbados or whatever; and then I would see someone coming down who was working for bread. It was just an instinct. I always knew when a woman was facing hard times. I became more aware of other women and didn't feel as isolated.

I have learned a lot through the harder times – such as, these things do come to you in life and it isn't because you deserve it, it isn't a punishment. It was a big change to feel that I wasn't bad and I wasn't a wrong person and didn't have to suffer all the confession things that go through your head. It wasn't of my own doing. Even if I had smacked my kids, and days when I screamed and ranted and raved and lost it, and days when I got out of the wrong side of the bed, I was only human. I couldn't do this 'Mr and Mrs Bun the Baker's Wife' thing – Happy Families was only a card game; it wasn't real life.

The kitchens finished and nobody wanted to see the kitchen again after the strike – especially the men, what with the meat and two veg and the cake and the tins that had things in 'em that no one knew what it was. They'd had enough of it. But we said that we felt we wanted to carry on, so we cleared our books, because we had money left over because we didn't know when the strike was going to finish. We took a vote and agreed to buy equipment for a chest ward, because such a lot of miners ended up there, and half of it went to the campaign for justice for miners. We also bought equipment for a miners' home. I joined a writers' workshop and I was dead scared but I felt I wanted to do it. I thought, I am going to go for it.

I didn't know I was strong then, and now I know. It isn't that I am confrontational, but I can now recognise things in myself that I quite like. I do like the fact that I am strong, and that I get a lot of positive feedback from friends, and that I have got friends who are true. That is a special treasure; we are like a family. We can talk about each other like see what's she's done but you couldn't say that; I would challenge you if you said anything wrong about 'the women', and it always 'the women'.

We are sisters; we even sing 'Sisters' by the Beverley Sisters when we have had three or four sherries. A few of the women have died with cancer; we have all had scares, to be honest; there isn't one of us that is truly fit. Honestly, we did think about having special ties made at one point, because we have all had hysterectomies. We always visit each other. I could pick the phone up and say – I never have, thank God – that I need some help, and I know they will be there whatever it was I needed. And I didn't know these women before the strike; they were strangers. It is like a family. It is there for me. One of the lines in the women's song is, 'We are women, we are strong. Where women's liberation failed to move, this strike has mobilised.' I think that sums us up.

Mary is still on the campaign trail, and I got the distinct impression that she would continue to be a self-made activist until the day she 'popped her clogs'. After the early frustrations and disappointments in her life, she was not going to let go of something so precious as a purpose, a cause but, most of all, a sisterhood. Despite the barriers that were put in her way, Mary found her destiny and nothing would send her back to the land of dusters and depression.

Mary had worked hard to come to terms with how she had been treated by her mother. I felt that her ability to speak about it to me, a stranger, was part of her way of trying to lay the ghost to rest, although her obvious distress showed she was still having to work at it. Often, what we feel to be scary secrets that cannot be talked about and must be hidden lose their power when they are spoken out loud. So it was with Mary's relationship with her mother.

She had come up with a number of ways of coping with the more painful aspects of life. Laughter was one of them. She told me how, when she was younger, she would go to confession each week. Her mother had told her that it was a sin to 'touch yourself'. At the age of nine Mary couldn't understand how she was supposed to wash properly without touching herself. So she felt that each time she had a bath she was a sinner, and there was no way she would ask her mother about it.

When she told the priest in the confessional her sins for the week, she would always include '. . . and Father, forgive me because I touched myself'. Laughing, she says she did this for many years. It wasn't until she was in her thirties that she realised her mother had meant masturbation. So, for most of her life she had been saying penance for a sin she hadn't heard of, never mind committed.

Another way of dealing with her pain was to put it on paper.

I have always written things down because I couldn't open up to anyone. If I was at my lowest low I could get a piece of paper and I could write everything that was in my head. It didn't tell a story, it was just words. I mean it could have been 'Bastard, crying, sore, hurting, angry, cold . . .' – all sorts. I could write pages and pages of it. Sometimes it would turn into a story or a prayer and then I would crumple it up and stick it on the fire. It really worked for me and I have told others to try it. I say to many people, if you want to get something out, and sometimes it is really hard in life to find someone you would trust with your soul, but one way that is really good if you've got a worry is if you just write it all down on a piece of paper and you can eff and blind it as much as you like. You can put anything on that piece of paper because for that amount of time that you hold it, you can trust that piece of paper. Don't hide it or put it at the bottom of a drawer because it is still there, but if you burn it it's gone – whoosh – and that helps.

When I think about it, those words explained what had happened between us. She had treated talking to me as a similar exercise. She had opened up to me about the most intimate and painful details of her life and that had lightened her own load. The trouble was, she couldn't put a match to me. Her words would not go up in smoke this time; they would stand as her testimony, albeit anonymously.

The very fact that they sit on the page without a name reveals more than if they had been claimed by the real Mary. She asked to read the extract about herself before publication and decided to show her children, to see what they thought. I wonder whether she was looking for someone else to take responsibility for the washing of dirty linen, or perhaps she just wanted them to know what she had been through. But they were angry and upset that she had chosen to speak to the world and not to them about her life. They felt she came across as a thief and a mother who hit her children, that it didn't make the family look good. Having read the story, you can judge this for yourselves.

They were shocked that she had been so unhappy. Clearly, they had no idea their mother had suffered so much in her life. Mary told me all this on the phone in tears; she had waited until her husband had gone out before calling. She hadn't dared show him what had been written.

Mary is a woman stalked by the dark shadows of her past. She has come closer to finding herself and her independence, in large part thanks to the strike. She has helped many other women along the way by sharing the harsh lessons she learned, although I can't help but feel that, for Mary, there is still a great distance to cover before she really comes into her own. Her journey is far from over.

CHAPTER EIGHT

Whatever Next?
Women Against Pit Closures

For the women who embraced the industrial action, there were numerous consequences. As you have read, it gave them a fresh perspective on their lives and themselves. Certainly their actions brought with them a degree of kudos – a new respect from others in their community. Also gratitude for the help they gave. The movement was spontaneous; it was not anticipated by the government, nor even the NUM. You could not have planned this mass uprising of previously non-politicised wives, mothers and daughters. The women effectively bridged the male/female divide in areas where it had never before been challenged. They were transformed from "er indoors' to working-class heroes; although they cringe if you say as much in front of them. Their success attracted powerful females from other walks of life such as academics and professionals. The mining women achieved a political status denied many others by dint of the fact that they were on the front line of what was regarded as a true working-class battle for jobs. Just as they learned about politics the hard but quick way, they were also on a fast track to acceptance in the male-dominated world of trade unions.

To this day, a lot of these women do not see themselves as activists. They say they were just doing what they had to in order to survive. The coalfield women made their mark; they were the surprise result of the strike – the other outcomes were predictable. Inevitably, there was a price to pay, whether it was through broken marriages, lost jobs or unrealistic dreams.

There was one high-profile lady whom I got to know well during the strike and who was initially keen to become involved with this book. In the end, though, she felt she could not go ahead with telling her intimate story in detail. At first she was too unwell to take part. She wanted to spend what time she had left with her family. Second, she did not see eye to eye with some of the other women. There had been a falling out years ago and she couldn't let it pass. I have removed any identification of her but included her story in brief, as I feel it highlights some of the themes in this book.

This woman, a miner's wife I will call Jo, became a well-known face in her locality. When the strike began, she was among the first to realise women had a key role to play. Without knowing what the consequences would be, she pushed herself to the fore. She was a natural organiser and spokesperson. Early on, her phone began to ring off the hook with local reporters wanting an interview; newspapers did features on her; TV news crews were often crowded into her tiny front room sipping tea, while she gave them chapter and verse. Her face appeared on the cover of magazines. Her words were treated as gospel, hungrily scribbled down and reported. Jo became something of a celebrity in her area. It wasn't all positive, though. There were those who were jealous of her because of all the attention she was receiving. This led to a rift with some women – especially as Jo had no qualms about speaking her mind, no matter who she upset.

She did not let her detractors get in her way. She had found her mission in life and dedicated herself to 'the cause'. She went to all the major protests, organised fund-raising, the distribution of monies and food to those in need. For that year, she never had a moment to sit quietly and think about what was going on. Once journalists discover someone who can speak in sound bites about their cause, they put them high on the list of people to call for reaction to the latest development. This meant Jo was appearing regularly in local and national press reports.

The nature of the media is that ordinary people can find themselves taken from obscurity and transformed overnight into news celebrities. Generally, the attention doesn't last, and they quickly slip back into the shadows. But Jo found herself a media star for a year, long enough to believe it might last. For her, the continual feed of adrenaline and excitement had a profound impact. She not only became accustomed to having her say, but grew to love it. A role was created for women to speak, and she embraced it. She did a good job as well. Her words were powerful and solid. She didn't fall into any traps set for her, such as criticising the NUM leadership when the going got particularly tough. She became a consummate performer in front of the camera and microphone.

The ephemeral nature of the news means that stories, no matter how big, do not last. News organisations have a short attention span; they quickly get bored with running variations on the same story. Remember a few years ago when, every day we were bombarded with stories about AIDS and how it was going to kill millions in a terrifying pandemic? Yet now it hardly gets a mention, written about only when someone famous dies from it.

So when the men went back to work at the collieries, the story that had been such a frenzied media turn-on was switched off. The outside broadcast units were recalled to London along with the reporters, and we all moved on to the next assignment. This left Jo hanging in the air – a voice without a microphone, an activist without a cause. If I hadn't been so caught up in my own life, I might have given Jo a bit more thought but she didn't come to mind until a few years ago when I came across her number in an old contacts book. I wondered how she was getting on, and gave her a call.

I don't know what I was expecting. I suppose I thought she would have settled back into life and grown accustomed to the changes wrought by the strike. Perhaps she would have made the most of the lessons she had learned as a media personality. What I was not prepared for was to find her so altered and crushed by what had happened. She was in the depths of depression. She explained that the strike was the best but also, ultimately, the worst thing that had happened to her. Like so many others, she got a great buzz from appearing in the media. Those moments of fame were costly. The action was over, the spotlight switched off; the reporters no longer hounded her for her opinion, the phone was still. She had become headline news overnight, just as quickly she was dumped and forgotten. Her 'friends' in the press no longer returned her calls.

She drifted back onto the sidelines to watch helplessly as the local pits closed. Whereas the drama of the strike had fed the news appetite, the slow painful closure of collieries and the communities they supported attracted little coverage. In defeat the world didn't seem to care much about the fate of the miners and their families. Jo told me that, from her bedroom window, she used to be able to see the winding gear of a colliery. It wasn't a pretty view, but it represented jobs and income. Not long after the strike, the pit was demolished, the land flattened, grassed over, planted with ornamental trees and used as a park. It made the view more pleasant, but Jo felt it was sinister – the landscaping used to hide the past. There was no trace of what lay beneath.

She couldn't cope with her loss – not just of the pits but of the profile. She had been a somebody and couldn't face reverting back to being a nobody. Jo told me she had had a 'breakdown' and ended up on a psychiatric ward. This happened not long after the strike ended, but years later she still had not come to terms with what had happened to her.

The strike destroyed her life because it awoke a desire in her that she could not fulfil once the action was over. Jo found a purpose only to lose it again. She became aware of a world that she desperately wanted but could not hang onto.

Her story has a particular resonance as it is not unique. In varying degrees, it is something that happened to a large number of people in the mining communities – men and women. They had their moments of 'fame' and found it difficult or even impossible to settle back into a normal life. Fame, no matter how transient, can be a malign condition. Of course, journalists returned to the scene at regular intervals. Anniversaries are always attractive as they give news organisations what is known as a 'peg' – a reason for taking another look at a story some time after it has taken place. There is the first anniversary, then the fifth, tenth and twentieth, and so on. It provides an opportunity to take stock of events and see what the long-term impact was. It also helps fill column inches and slots of yawningly long news programmes. The twentieth anniversary was therefore an important time. It prompted many articles and broadcasts. In the process, deep-rooted feelings buried since the strike were resurrected.

One group who had been preparing for the anniversary for some years was WAPC; perhaps that is why it was easier to track them down than representatives of the NUM. The numbers I had for the union were either out of service or had answerphones that directed you to somewhere else that also had an answermachine. The union still exists but inevitably it faded with the closure of the pits. WAPC, on the other hand, appears to have held its ground. There is a hard core of women who refuse to slip quietly into the twilight. You will have read about some of them in this book. They continue to fight on a number of fronts, the main one being for the survival of what is left of the coal industry, and to encourage the use of coal instead of nuclear power.

WAPC is very much on the ball. It launched a new website in the spring of 2005. One of its key aims is to create an archive, by allowing women to tell their own stories. It also acts as a link to like-minded organisations around the world. WAPC has always attracted global interest, from Chilean freedom fighters to American mine workers. The group was also called in to advise on a major TV drama that documented events from the perspective of the mining communities. In March 2005 the programme, called Faith, was broadcast on BBC1. It was about two sisters, one married to a miner on strike, the other to a policeman. It followed the escalation of the dispute and the concurrent deterioration of the relationships between the two couples. The drama prompted criticism from the Tories, who said it was totally partial and unbalanced. Certainly, the Thatcher government and the police were not shown in a good light; but those who were there would argue that that was the reality at the time. Not surprisingly, the programme went down well with the former mining communities; the team who produced it went to great pains to get to know the people. Some of the cast attended an anniversary weekend organised by WAPC, and apparently had their eyes opened to the miners' view of events. Previously their ideas had been based on what they had read and seen on TV news bulletins.

One of the WAPC women said to me that the mining families were made to look like thugs and violent law-breakers. Certainly, some of the demonstrators were like that but the majority of those caught up in the dispute were ordinary people. Far from being the 'enemy within', they would now be euphemistically labelled 'collateral damage' in a war between two powerful superegos. As history is busily rewriting itself about the miners' past, the future is also unclear. Once a pit is closed it cannot easily be reopened. Old shafts become sterile and are of no use; they have to be filled in. New shafts have to be sunk, and the cost is considerable. But as I write there are an increasing number of articles appearing in the press about the possible revival of coal. We are running out of gas, and imports of the black stuff are becoming expensive. Could we see the day when King Coal is resurrected, in part at least? The chorus of 'I told you so' would be deafening.

So what of Queen Coal? Unlike King Coal, she didn't disappear after the strike. She has outlived the old pits and refuses to be shooed back to the kitchen. After my journey revisiting these women and charting their lives, I am left with one particularly strong image. It is a mental picture, painted for me by one of them, of how she imagined the future. Her group would still be together, this 'sisterhood', but in an old people's home. They would be grey-haired and wrinkly, sitting in wheelchairs, showing their knickers and having a laugh like naughty children at the back of a classroom. They would give the long-suffering staff hell, by not doing as they were told and by giving them some lip. Their bodies might bow to the years, but they would be as feisty as ever. Looking deeper into the crystal ball, Queen Coal would see a time when they had all 'shuffled off' to the great soup kitchen in the sky. Death held no regrets for them; they knew they would be leaving a worthwhile legacy.

The stories of their lives and the fight they pursued for so many years would inspire the next generation of women, encouraging them not to fall into the traps that came in the guise of 'tradition'. She believed that what the mining women went through would help them look for and discover their inner strengths, no matter how deeply buried these traits were by their upbringing. She said she was certain the spirit of Queen Coal would live on. With that, she laughed and began to recite the campaign song that had accompanied her and her 'sisters' through the years:

Queen Coal

We are women, we are strong,
We are fighting for our lives
Side by side with our men
Who work the nation's mines,
United by the struggle,
United by the past,
And it's – Here we go! Here we go!
For the women of the working class.

Bibliography

The Miners' Strike 1984–85 in Pictures, New Park Publications, Old Town, Clapham, London, 1985.

We Struggled to Laugh, Barnsley Miners' Wives Action Group, Sheffield Women's Printing Co-op, 1987.

Women Against Pit Closures, Barnsley Women Against Pit Closures, 1984.

Fitzpatrick, Denise, Nelson, Christine M., Cadwallader, May and Armitage, Edith, *Ten Years on and Still Laughing*, 1994.

Keating, Jackie, *Counting the Cost*, Wharncliffe Publishing Ltd, Barnsley, South Yorkshire, 1991.

Index

Index